PLURAL+PLUS

COMPANION WEBSITE

Purchase of *Functional Phonetics Workbook, Third Edition* comes with complimentary access to audio files on a PluralPlus companion website. The audio files are available on both the companion website and the accompanying CDs so the user can choose the format that best suits their needs. The content is identical on both.

The companion website is located at:

http://www.pluralpublishing.com/publication/fpw3e

To access the audio files, you must register on the companion website and log in using the access code below.

Access Code: FPW3E-NYDTAW

Functional Phonetics Workbook

Third Edition

Functional Phonetics Workbook

Third Edition

Mary Lou Marsoun Cancio, MA, CCC-SLP
Sadanand Singh, PhD

PLURAL
PUBLISHING
INC.

5521 Ruffin Road
San Diego, CA 92123

email: information@pluralpublishing.com
website: http://www.pluralpublishing.com

ISBN-13: 978-1-63550-005-9
ISBN-10: 1-63550-005-2

Contents

Preface

The *Functional Phonetics Workbook* was designed to be used in several ways. It is a valuable classroom resource for instructors who teach an introductory phonetics course. It can be used, with the accompanying audio files, by individuals as they learn the International Phonetic Alphabet (IPA) who may not have access to formal instruction. The *Functional Phonetics Workbook* also provides a convenient review format for those who require a review of their phonetic transcription skills. For example, this might be a first-semester clinician who has not reviewed phonetics since taking their introductory class of communicative disorders courses. The student may find it a helpful review if they have been assigned an articulation or phonological process-disorder client.

The *Workbook* focuses on the basics of phonetic transcription in Standard American English. In addition, for students who are learning English as a second language, this workbook is a valuable learning resource. Students should find the Phoneme Study Cards a very helpful study tool for learning the IPA sound/symbol association. All of these cards can be listened to on the audio files. Each audio file corresponds to the Phoneme Study Card number.

New material added to the third edition includes Listening Activities that provide students with an opportunity to hear the contrast between phonemes. A helpful chart for Place-Manner-Voicing has been added, as well as a list of Internet resources. The audio files are now available on both CDs and a PluralPlus companion website. The workbook comes with access to both so the user can choose the format that best suits their needs.

The *Workbook* remains a helpful basic resource to master use of the IPA. Having taught an introductory Phonetics course since 1994 has refined my view of the basics required for students to become competent transcribers. The success of hundreds of students as they become proficient using the IPA has brought great satisfaction. Enjoy the learning process!

Mary Lou Marsoun, MA, CCC-SLP

Acknowledgements

The memory of Dr. Sadanand Singh, co-author for the first edition remains. I have fond memories of Dr. Thayne Hedges who instilled my love of Phonetics when I took his course as an undergraduate.

Thanks to the Plural Publishing Group.

This edition would not be possible without the help and support of the Wing Family —Pam, Kevin, and Isaac (he is the most well-behaved six year old I've ever seen!). Cheryl Andrews' innovative page format continues to be a unique feature of the text. The original recordings by Kimberly Lenz, Andrew Sessions, Scott Calderwood, and Kevin Wing have been a continued helpful source. In addition, thanks again to Kevin who agreed to record the Listening Activities for this edition.

Ray Settle and Eric Sherbon of Maximus Recording Studios have again made the recording process run smoothly.

This edition is dedicated to my dear daughter, Mary Claire and her husband, Ian Bachman. As always, love to the Marsoun clan and my friends who continue to put up with me.

Mary Lou Marsoun

Workbook Format

For each phoneme, an exercise to help you determine initial-medial-final phoneme position is provided, including the transcription exercise number and corresponding audio file. Remember that not all of the words in these exercises contain the specified phoneme. The goal is to ensure the student is not confused by spelling, and to focus on listening to the *sound* of the phonemes in the word. A phonetic transcription exercise follows, with a reference to the Phoneme Study Card and audio file.

The audio files are available on both the accompanying CDs and a PluralPlus companion website (the URL and access code is available on the inside front cover of the workbook). The workbook comes with access to both options so the user can choose the format that best suits their needs. The content is identical on both. The audio files are identified by the CD number located on (1, 2, 3, or 4), and are similarly organized into four sections on the companion website.

A phoneme description page is provided for the IPA phonemes. Each page is organized to provide the following information (see example on next page): (1) description of place, manner, and listing of distinctive features, (2) vocal fold and velopharyngeal port position, (3) tongue position and how the phoneme is produced, (4) variations in spelling, (5) word position in Standard American English (SAE), and (6) clinical information. The Clinical Information section includes a listing of a consonant cognate (sound made in the same place and the same manner), common articulatory substitutions (replacement of one phoneme for another), or omission (absence of a phoneme and another phoneme does not replace it).

A Crossword Puzzle and Word Search are also included, and provide more practice in phonetic transcription. Answers to all of the Crossword Puzzles and Word Searches are listed in Appendix B: Answers to Exercises.

Example of the Phoneme Description Page

Distinctive Features	Tongue Position
1.	3.
Voicing/Velopharyngeal Port	**Spelling Variations**
2.	4.
Word Position	**Clinical Information**
5.	6.

1

The International Phonetic Alphabet (IPA)

Learning Objectives

After reading this chapter, you will be able to:

1. State why the International Phonetic Alphabet (IPA) was developed.

2. Name and explain three reference points for studying speech sounds.

3. Define Phonetics and explain why it is a functional tool.

4. Identify the origin of many of the symbols of the IPA.

The English have no respect for their language, and will not teach their children to speak it. They cannot spell it because they have nothing to spell it with but an old foreign alphabet of which only the consonants—and not all of them— have any agreed speech value. Consequently no man can teach himself what it should sound like from reading it . . .

—George Bernard Shaw, Preface to *Pygmalion*

As George Bernard Shaw laments, the "old foreign alphabet" does not provide a reliable sound-symbol representation of speech sounds.

In 1886, the International Phonetic Association developed a sound-symbol system based on an earlier alphabet developed by British phonetician Henry Sweet. This system was to be used to represent the sounds of all the languages of the world, and provided phoneticians with a system to communicate with each other.

If our spoken speech could accurately be represented by the English alphabet, we would have no need for a phonetic alphabet. Let's take a brief look at how we spell and pronounce some common English words. Although we have only some 40 sounds in English, we have more than 200 ways of spelling them, using our alphabet. For example, the sound of "sh" has up to 14 different spellings (faction, shoot, sugar, mission, ocean, champagne, etc.), the long "o" sound can be represented by over a dozen spellings (crow, so, doe, beau, etc.), and the long "a" sound in our alphabet is represented by 12 different spellings (lay, take, maid, freight, great, hey, etc.). Many consonants also are represented in several different ways. Consider the spelling of "t" in thank, tender, notion, the "h" in ache, hoist, hour, three, and enough, and the "c" in chair, bloc, and citrus. Although there has been a constant push from various groups to regularize our spelling, these movements have been met with resistance for centuries. You can see that mastery of the phonetic alphabet is an absolute necessity for anyone who needs an unambiguous, one-to-one representation of spoken speech. The phonetic alphabet meets this need.

Phonetic symbols are placed in slash marks, or virgules, such as /k/. Brackets [ ] are used to indicate a group of connected speech sounds.

Many consonant symbols of the IPA originate from the Roman alphabet: p, b, t, d, k, g, l, m, n, r, f, v, s, z, and w. Other symbols are from the Greek alphabet or have been created especially for the IPA. The "x" is not found in the IPA and is represented by /ks/, as "q" is represented by /kw/. Similarly, the "c" is represented by a /k/ in words with a "k" sound.

The Greek capital Theta /θ/ is used for the voiceless "th" as in "**th**igh." The /ð/ represents the voiced "th" as in "**th**is." An upside down "w" /ʍ/ or /hw/ is used for the voiceless "wh" as in "**wh**eat."

A lengthened sigmoid /ʃ/ represents the "sh" as in "**sh**ip." The /ʒ/ symbolizes the "zh" sound, as in "bei**ge**." The IPA combines the symbols /t/ and /ʃ/ into /tʃ/ for the "ch" sound, as in "**ch**ick." Similarly, the /d/ and /ʒ/ join for /dʒ/ as in "**J**ack." The symbol /ŋ/ represents the "ng" sound, as in "ri**ng**." The /j/ may look familiar to you, but in the IPA it is used to represent the "y" sound as in "**y**oung." IPA symbols for English consonants are shown in Table 1–1.

The vowels of the IPA may be considered more challenging than the consonants, as you must learn a new sound/symbol system for the majority of them. For instance, the "a, e, i, u" do not represent the traditional vowel sounds. In addition, the IPA uses /ɪ/ /ʊ/ /æ/ /ɛ/ /ɝ/ /ɚ/ /ʌ/ /ə/ /ɔ/. You will be relieved to learn that the "o" is represented by the familiar /o/ in the IPA, although some phoneticians use the /oʊ/ to represent "o." As you can see, the vowels of the IPA can be confusing. Similarly, the diphthongs present another sound difference. The diphthongs are written as a combination of two vowel sounds fused together, for example, the /aɪ/ in the word "island." Other diphthongs include /aʊ/ as in "**ou**t," /ɔɪ/ as in "**coy**," and /ju/ as in "**cu**te." IPA symbols for English vowels and diphthongs are shown in Table 1–2.

You are learning a new, exciting language—it will take time and study, but your efforts will be rewarded as you master transcription with the IPA!

Why Is It Important to Study Phonetics?

Phonetics, the study of speech sounds, is an extremely useful (and mandatory!) tool for the speech-language pathologist. *The International Phonetic Alphabet* (IPA) is used

Table 1–1. English Consonants and Their IPA Symbols

Primary Allographic or Orthographic Symbol	IPA Symbol	Key Words
p	/p/	pal, apart, tap
b	/b/	barn, cabin, rub
t	/t/	tea, water, aunt
d	/d/	dish, lady, sand
k	/k/	card, bacon, hook
g	/g/	game, sugar, bag
f	/f/	feed, afford, elf
v	/v/	van, envy, have
th	/θ/	thin, something, cloth
th	/ð/	this, weather, bathe
s	/s/	sat, lesson, horse
z	/z/	zone, puzzle, hose
sh	/ʃ/	ship, fashion, mash
zh	/ʒ/	treasure, beige
h	/h/	hit, behave
wh	/hw/	which, nowhere
ch	/tʃ/	chip, scratching, pitch
j	/dʒ/	jam, magic, page
w	/w/	wet, sandwich
y	/j/	yard, beyond
l	/l/	leaf, mellow, hill
r	/r/	rake, carrot, or
m	/m/	men, camel, time
n	/n/	net, dinner, pine
ng	/ŋ/	ringer, ring

to transcribe, or record using the IPA, the speech of a client. Transcribing the speech errors of a child or adult is an integral part of the assessment process.

Transcription can be *phonemic* or *phonetic*. Phonemic transcription is broad transcription. Broad transcription converts speech into phonemic symbols, written within virgules / /. Phonetic transcription is narrow transcription that records exactly how an utterance was produced. Narrow transcription utilizes diacritics (see Chapter 15), indicating a specific way a phoneme was produced. Words are written inside of brackets [ ].

Recording the client's speech using the IPA enables another professional to identify how speech sounds have been produced.

Table 1–2. English Vowels and Their IPA Symbols

Primary Allographic or Orthographic Symbol	IPA Symbol	Key Words
ee	/i/	eat, keep, free
-i-	/ɪ/	in, mitt, city
-e-	/ɛ/	ebb, net
-a-	/æ/	at, bat, ham
a-e	/e/	age, face, say
-ur-	/ɝ/ (stressed)	earn, herd, fur
	/ɚ/ (unstressed)	herder, percent
-u-	/ʌ/ (stressed)	up, cup, done
	/ə/ (unstressed)	alive, relative, sofa
-oo-	/u/	boot, stew, soup
-oo-	/ʊ/	hood, could, cook
-aw-	/ɔ/	all, yawn, paw
-o-	/ɑ/	on, bomb
oa	/o/	oak, pole, toe
ou	/aʊ/	ouch, gown, how
i-e	/aɪ/	ice, shine, rye
oi	/ɔɪ/	oyster, loin, toy
u	/ju/	use, cue, mew

How Speech Sounds Can Be Studied

One of the ways that speech sounds can be studied is as isolated, separate, and independent entities. Another way speech sounds can be studied is by comparing one sound with another sound. In this Workbook, we will discuss the system of speech sounds classified as Standard American English (SAE), the major dialect of English spoken in the United States of America. Refer to Chapter 16 for a definition of SAE.

A detailed study of speech sounds involves three reference points: (a) the organs that produce speech, and their function in producing speech sounds (*physiological phonetics*), (b) the physical properties of the individual speech sounds (*acoustic phonetics*), and (c) the process by which the individual speech sounds are perceived and identified (*perceptual phonetics*). Physiological phonetics is the focus of this Workbook, and is discussed in Chapter 2.

Regardless of the setting in which a speech-language pathologist is employed, a thorough knowledge of phonetics is essential. For instance, it is not uncommon for a speech-language pathologist employed in a school setting to use phonetics daily. Considering the importance of phonetics as a functional tool, it has always puzzled the author that only one semester of undergraduate phonetics is required for academic majors in speech-language pathology in the United States. In the United Kingdom, four courses in phonetics are required!

STUDY QUESTIONS

1. Why is mastery of the International Phonetic Alphabet (IPA) important?

The mastery of the IPA is important because the normal alphabet does not show the different sounds that each letter produces

2. From what language did many of the IPA symbols originate?

Greek & Roman

3. What is the purpose of the IPA?

To represent sounds that the normal alphabet cannot

4. Why are the IPA vowels considered more challenging than the consonants?

The IPA vowels are considered more challenging than the consonants because you must learn a new sound/symbol for most of them.

5. Define Phonetics.

The study and classification of speech sounds.

6. Name and describe the three reference points in the study of speech sounds.

Organs that produce sound & their function - physiological
Physical properties in the individual speech sounds - acoustic
Process by which the sounds are perceived & identified - perceptual

7. Write the IPA phoneme that represents the following sounds:

a. "sh" ʃ
b. "th" θ and ð
c. "ng" ŋ

d. "ee" i
e. schwa ə
f. "ash" æ

8. What is the difference between *phonemic* and *phonetic* transcription?

Phonemic is broad & converts speech into phonemic symbols using virgules, phonetic is narrow & records exactly how an utterance was produced

2

Learning to Write IPA Symbols: Syllables and Word Shapes

Learning Objectives

After reading this chapter, you will be able to:

1. Define a syllable and its components.

2. Explain the difference between a closed and open syllable.

3. Define Initial-Medial-Final consonant position.

4. State why it is essential to write IPA symbols correctly.

5. Write consonants, vowels, and diphthongs of IPA correctly.

Studying this chapter will help you familiarize yourself with the symbols of the IPA, as well as how to write them correctly. The only way to become comfortable with writing the unfamiliar symbols is to practice, practice, practice! In addition, exercises are provided to learn the distinction between the spelling of a word (orthography), and how that word *sounds*.

An important part of learning phonetics is the ability to identify the position of a phoneme in a word. Terms used to describe the position of a sound in a word vary. Words can be divided into syllables, with "V" indicating a vowel and "C" indicating a consonant. For example, the word "sold" is a one-syllable word with the CVCC classification. An example of a two-syllable word is "soda," which would be identified as CVCV.

Consonants have been viewed as appearing in one of three positions in a word: at the beginning of a word (*initial position*) or the first sound heard, the middle of a word (*medial position*), and at the end of a word *(final position)*, or the last sound heard. Another classification system identifies a consonant that occurs *before* a vowel, as a *prevocalic* consonant, one that occurs *between* two vowels as an *intervocalic* consonant, and a consonant that occurs *following* a vowel as a *postvocalic* consonant. Locate the /l/ phoneme in the words "look," "alone," and "cool":

Initial Position or Prevocalic: look

Medial Position or Intervocalic: alone

Final Position or Postvocalic: cool

The prevocalic and postvocalic classification system is useful in classifying the position of consonant clusters. A *cluster*, also known as a *blend*, is two or more consonants within the same syllable. These can occur in prevocalic or postvocalic positions. Table 3–5 in Chapter 3 provides examples of consonant clusters.

Recently, consonant locations have been described in terms of their functions, rather than their specific location in a word. Consonants can be viewed as performing only two functions, *releasing* vowels or *arresting* vowels. In the word "soap," the consonant /s/ releases the vowel /o/, whereas the consonant /p/ stops or arrests the vowel.

Bernthal and Bankson (1998) specify the *initial, medial, final* word position as the system used most often for sound-position descriptors. In this workbook, an initial, medial, and final identification exercise has been provided for each IPA phoneme. The words in these exercises were selected to increase your listening ability and to reinforce the difference between the way a word is spelled and how it is pronounced. You will find that the specific phoneme may not always occur in the word examples. These exercises can be heard on the audio files. Students who are learning English as a second language should find these exercises particularly useful.

Learning to Write IPA Symbols: Syllables and Word Shapes

One goal of this chapter is to teach the student how to write the symbols of the IPA correctly, as well as the sound/symbol association, which is the foundation of phonetics.

Directions for Phoneme Study Card Use

The Phoneme Study Cards that accompany this book are an essential tool in the mastery of the sound/symbol association of the International Phonetic Alphabet.

Each card is numbered. Corresponding numbers are cited in the Transcription Exercises to help identify the phoneme. You can also listen to the pronunciation of the Phoneme Study Card on the audio files.

Here are some suggestions for using these cards:

- Learn the **sound** of the IPA phoneme shown on the front of the card. Remember that you can listen to the sounds pronounced on the audio files.

- Memorize the phonetic description for each phoneme.

- Become familiar with the word-position examples.

- Create phonetically transcribed words by using the cards.

- Challenge yourself to reduce the amount of time it takes to identify the sound of each phoneme.

- Drill, drill, drill!

Following are examples of IPA phonemes. The phoneme is handwritten for you and you can practice writing the phoneme in the space provided.

The "Familiar" IPA Consonants

It is *essential* that you write the symbols of the IPA correctly. If you do not write the symbols correctly, another professional will not be able to read your transcription (Figure 2–1). This is critical because all your referrals to yourself during reassessment and treatment, or to your professional colleagues, or to your supervisors must reflect the same information.

"P/p" is written as   p

"B/b" is written as   b

"K/k" is written as   k

"G/g" is written as   g

"T/t" is written as   t

"D/d" is written as   d

"S/s" is written as   s

"Z/z" is written as   z

"W/w" is written as   w

"F/f" is written as   f

"V/v" is written as   v

"R/r" is written as   r

"J/j" is written as   j

"H/h" is written as   h

"L/l" is written as   l

"M/m" is written as   m

"N/n" is written as   n

Figure 2–1. Familiar IPA consonants.

The "Unfamiliar" IPA Consonants

These consonants may seem very strange, but you will become more at ease with them as you continue your study of phonetics (Figure 2–2).

The Vowels of the IPA

The vowels of the IPA may seem confusing at first, but practice will help (Figure 2–3)! Remember: Do not be confused by spelling, but keep in mind the *sound* of the vowel.

How Do I Write the /æ/ (ash)?

1 First, write the schwa /ə/, starting at the top of the letter (Figure 2–4).

2 Without lifting your pencil from the paper, continue writing the letter "e."

"sh" as in "*sh*ip" is written as   ʃ

"zh" as in "bei*g*e" is written as   ʒ

"th" as in "*th*in" is written as   θ

"th" as in "*th*is" is written as   ð

"ng" as in "si*ng*" is written as   ŋ

"ch" as in "*ch*urch" is written as   tʃ

"j" as in "*j*am" is written as   dʒ

Figure 2–2. Unfamiliar IPA consonants.

The short "i" as in "zip" is written as ___ɪ___ _____

The long "e" as in "keep" is written as ___i___ _____

The short "e" as in "bet" is written as ___ɛ___ _____

The short "a" as in "cat" is written as ___æ___ _____

The long "a" as in "ape" is written as ___e___ _____

The "ah" sound as in "sod" is written as ___ɑ___ _____

The "uh" sound as in "cup" is written as ___ʌ___ _____

The schwa as in "*a*bout" is written as ___ə___ _____

The "oo" as in "soup" is written as ___u___ _____

The "oo" as in "c*oo*k" is written as ___ʊ___ _____

The "o" as in "boat" is written as ___o___ _____

The "aw" as in "paw" is written as ___ɔ___ _____

The "er" as in "h*er*d" is written as ___ɜ___ _____

The "er" as in "herd*er*" is written as ___ɚ___ _____

Figure 2–3. Vowels of the IPA.

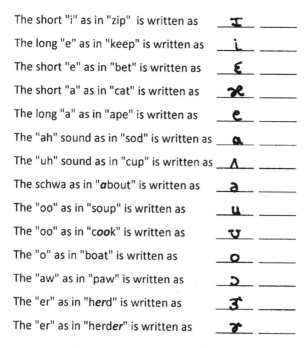

1. ə   ∂   2. æ   æ

Figure 2–4. Writing the ash.

The Diphthongs of the IPA

The diphthongs present their own unique challenge because two vowels are used. In addition, the diphthongs are written with a slur (‿) beneath them (Figure 2–5). It is important to write the "a" of the diphthongs correctly. Figure 2–6 will help you.

Syllables

An important part of learning phonetics is the ability to identify the position of a phoneme in a word. Syllables comprise words. Peña-Brooks and Hegde (2007) state that children and adults can identify syllables in words, but cannot define a syllable. A syl-

"ie" as in "p*ie*" is written as ___aɪ___ _____

"ou" as in "c*ow*" is written as ___aʊ___ _____

"oy" as in "b*oy*" is written as ___ɔɪ___ _____

"u" as in "v*iew*" is written as ___ju___ _____

Figure 2–5. Diphthongs of the IPA.

How to Write the Capped /a/ Used in Diphthongs

1 Write the curved line.

2 Add the half circle.

1: ⌐↲

2: ϛC

Completed: a   ɑ

- Add the /ɪ/ and a diphthong to make the rising low front to high front off-glide diphthong: aɪ

- Add the /ʊ/ and a diphthong to make the rising low front to high back off-glide diphthong: aʊ

Figure 2–6. How to write the /a/.

lable can be formed by one *vowel, diphthong,* or *syllabic consonant* (see Chapter 5 regarding syllabic consonants). In addition, a *consonant* and vowel or diphthong can form a syllable. Vowels and diphthongs are produced by an unobstructed breath stream. Consonants are formed with an obstructed, or partially obstructed vocal tract. A syllable includes the *onset* (a consonant that releases the *nucleus* of the syllable) and the *rhyme*. The rhyme consists of two parts, that is the nucleus (vowel), plus the *coda* or consonant that is added at the end of the vowel. For example, for the word "sat" (consisting of one syllable), the onset is the consonant /s/, and the rhyme consists of the nucleus vowel /æ/, plus the coda or consonant /t/. It is convenient to call the consonant /s/ the *releaser* of the nucleus vowel and /t/ the *arrester* of the nucleus vowel. In addition, syllables can be closed (containing a coda) or open (no coda).

Here's a trivia question: What entertainment icon dropped a syllable from her name before she became famous? Answer: Barbara (Bar-ba-ra) Streisand eliminated a syllable to become Barbra (Bar-bra) (Mann, 2012).

Table 2–1 provides examples of different types of syllables.

Here are some words divided into syllables to study as examples:

1. phone   (1)
2. phoneme   (2) phon-eme
3. phonetics   (3) pho-net-ics
4. phonetician (4) pho-ne-ti-cian
5. university   (5) un-i-vers-i-ty

Table 2–1. Syllables

		RHYME (Vowel and Coda)			
		Onset (Consonant Before Vowel)	Nucleus (Vowel)	Coda (Consonant After Vowel)	Orthographic
Phonetic Transcription	1.	p	æ	n	pan (1)
	2.	s	i		sea (2)
	3.		ɪ	t	it (1)
	4.	spr	ɪ	ŋ	spring (1)
	5.	p	ɔ		paw (2)
	6.	θ	ɑ	t	thought (1)
	7.	skr	i	tʃ	screech (1)
	8.		a͡ɪ		I (2)
	9.	n	a͡ʊ		now (2)
	10.	t	ʌ	f	tough (1)

(1) = Closed syllables (contains coda).
(2) = Open syllable (contains no coda).

Exercise 2–A

Now it's your turn. Divide these words into syllables. (Answers in Appendix B)

		Syllable Division	# Syllables
1.	coda	co-da	2
2.	nucleus	nu-cle-us	3
3.	vowel	vow-el	2
4.	syllable	syl-la-ble	3
5.	rhyme	rhyme	1
6.	initial	i-ni-tial	3
7.	medial	me-di-al	3
8.	final	fi-nal	2
9.	blend	blend	1
10.	cluster	clus-ter	2
11.	arresting	a-rrest-ing	3
12.	releasing	re-leas-ing	3
13.	consonant	con-son-ant	3
14.	orthography	or-tho-graph-y	4
15.	pound	pound	1
X 16.	wiggle	wiggle wig-gle	1
17.	intelligence	in-tell-i-gence	4
18.	mathematical	math-e-mat-i-cal	5
19.	centimeter	cent-i-me-ter	4
20.	chocolate	choc-o-late	3

Another system used to identify consonants and vowels in words is by using "C" for a consonant and "V" for a vowel. For example, the word "sold" is a one-syllable word with a CVCC classification. An example of a two-syllable word is "soda," with a CVCV classification. Table 2–2 provides examples of word syllable shapes.

Table 2–2. Word Syllable Shapes

Cluster: Two adjacent consonants in the same syllable				
sing:	C	V	C	
	s	ɪ	ŋ	
singing:	C	V	C	V	C
	s	ɪ	ŋ	ɪ	ŋ
sting:	C	C	V	C	
	s	t	ɪ	ŋ	
string:	C	C	C	V	C
	s	t	r	ɪ	ŋ

C = Consonant; **V** = Vowel.

Exercise 2–B

Provide the syllable shapes for these words. The first three have been completed for you. Check your answers in Appendix B.

What syllable shapes fit the following words?

1. ash — V C
2. crash — C C V C
3. splash — C C C V C
X 4. eastern — VCCCC VCCVC
5. green — CCVC
6. three — CCV
7. preach — CCVC
8. scream — CCCVC
9. frame — CCVC
10. phosphorus — CVCCVCVC

Exercise 2–C

Here's a challenge. Exercise 2–C lists dinosaur names. Put these in CV shapes. Answers in Appendix B.

What syllable shapes fit the following dinosaur names?

1. Brachyceratops — CCVCVCVCVCVCC
2. Corythosaurus — CVCVCVCVCVC
3. Dilophosaurus — CVCVCVCVCVC
4. Microceratops — CVCCVCVCVCVCC
5. Pachyrhinosaurus — CVCVCVCVCVCVS
6. Pentaceratops — CVCCVCVCVCVCC
7. Triceratops — CCVCVCVCVCC
8. Brachiosaurus — CCVCVVCVCVC
9. Epachthosaurus — VCVCCVCVCVC
10. Heterodontosaurus — CVCVCVCVCCVCVCVS
    CVCVVCV CCVCVCVC

Transcription Exercise 2–1    **AUDIO 1–2**

It is important that you develop the skill to determine the number of *sounds* contained in a word. Count how many sounds each word contains. Listen to AUDIO 1–2 to hear these words pronounced. The "Examples" section should be helpful to you.

Examples

noisy has 4 sounds: n ɔɪ z i
cough has 3 sounds: k ɑ f
together has 6 sounds: t u g ɛ ð ɚ
ship has 3 sounds: ʃ ɪ p
knife has 3 sounds: n ɑɪ f
giraffe has 4 sounds: dʒ ɚ æ f
baked has 4 sounds: b e k t
phantom has 6 sounds: f æ n t ə m
might has 3 sounds: m ɑɪ t

anniversary has 9 sounds: æ n ɪ v ɚ s ə r i
write has 3 sounds: r ɑɪ t
long has 3 sounds: l ɑ ŋ
Note: "ng" is transcribed: ŋ
whole has 3 sounds: h o l
"**x**" has 3 sounds: ɛ ks
measure has 4 sounds: m ɛ ʒ ɚ
gnat has 3 sounds: n æ t

Sounds		Transcription	
X 3 2	1. gnaw	[nɔ] ✓	
3	2. shape	[ʃep] ✓	
X 4 5	3. cousin	[kʌzɪn] ✓	
4	4. leisure	[liʒɚ] X liʒɚ	
X 4 3	5. tongue	[tʌn] X tʌŋ	
2	6. who	[hju] X hu	
4	7. rather	[ræðɚ] X r æðɚ	
3	8. tough	[tʌf] ✓	
3	9. kneel	[nil] ✓	
X 2 3	10. ax	[æks] ✓	
1	11. cinnamon	[sɪnʌmɪn] ✓	
3	12. wrap	[rəp] X r æp	
4	13. raked	[rekd] ✓	
3	14. sight	[sɑɪt] ✓	
5	15. phoneme	[tonem] X tonɪm	

Transcription Exercise 2–2

🔊 **AUDIO 1–3**

Phoneme Fill-In Exercise

Directions: Using the IPA, write the first *sound* in each of the following words:

1. push   p _____
2. real   r _____
3. act   æ _____
4. key   k _____
5. top   t _____
6. in   I _____
7. see   s _____
8. every   ɛ _____
9. very   v _____
10. urge   ɝ _____
11. easy   i _____
12. dog   d _____
13. able   e _____

Write the letters here, and then see what they spell:

præktɪsɛ vɝide

præktɪs ɛvɝide

Transcription Exercise 2–3

 **AUDIO 1–4**

Phoneme Identification Exercise

This introductory exercise in phoneme identification is designed to fine-tune your listening abilities. Listen to each word and write the phoneme common to each group of words in a row.

Remember—don't let spelling confuse you!

Consonants

					Phoneme
1. chorus	Quaker	mannequin	Zachary	physique	/_k_/ ✓
2. tango	kangaroo	Hong Kong	mingle	rectangle	/_g_/ ✗ ŋ
3. jumbo	effigy	geology	damage	fugitive	/_dʒ_/ ✓
4. phrase	raffle	tough	factory	Ralph	/_f_/ ✓
? 5. yesterday	papaya	Johann	bayou	savior	/_j_/
6. misery	hose	adviser	weighs	resume	/_z_/ ✓

Vowels

7. fruit	loop	tube	knew	zoos	/_u_/ ✓
8. eve	cease	free	quiche	beanie	/_i_/ ✓
9. coach	own	robe	beau	throw	/_o_/ ✓
10. birch	hermit	urge	myrtle	fur	/_ɝ_/ ✓
11. bathe	lay	vein	gate	eighty	/_e_/ ✓
12. ah	jaunt	spa	palm	shock	/_ɑ_/ ✓

YOUR FIRST EXERCISE—Transcribe Your Name!

Transcription Rules

Rule 1: Transcribe according to the way your name *sounds,* not how it is *spelled.*

Rule 2: No capital letters for your first, middle, or last name.

Rule 3: Put first, middle, and last names in one set of brackets: [ ].

Rule 4: No double phonetic symbols—remember, it is how your name sounds, not how many letters are used.

Helpful Hints

- Be sure to use the Phoneme Study Cards to help you make the sound-symbol connection.
- Your phonetics instructor can review your transcription and make helpful suggestions.

JUST FOR FUN

Transcribe the names of family members, pets, favorite actors, and sports figures.

kaitlyn

ketlin

Desiree

dɛzɪre

STUDY QUESTIONS

1. In word formations, what do "C" and "V" represent?

V represents vowel & C represents consonant

2. List and define three consonant positions in words.

initial, medial & final

3. Define prevocalic, intervocalic, and postvocalic.

Prevocalic: a consonant that occurs before a vowel, intervocalic: occurs between two vowels, postvocalic occurs after a vowel

4. Define nucleus, onset, and coda.

an onset (usually a consonant) appears before the nucleus, while a coda appears after, a nucleus is the central part of a syllable (usually a vowel)

5. What comprises a syllable?

Syllable: a segment of speech that consists of a vowel, with or without one or more accompanying consonants

6. Give an example of a closed and an open syllable.

ex) closed ... fan, left (ends with a consonant
ex) open ... pa-per, even, o-pen (not closed by a
(long-vowel)   consonant)

7. Give an example of a CCCVC word.

sirap

8. Define orthography.

conventional spelling system of a language

3

Articulatory Aspects of Phonetics

Learning Objectives

After reading this chapter, you will be able to:

1. Name the four processes of PARR.

2. Describe vocal fold position for abduction and adduction.

3. Explain difference between place and manner of phoneme production.

4. State the place and manner for all IPA consonants.

5. Define and give examples of syllable-initiating and syllable-terminating consonant clusters.

A review of basic anatomy and physiology is helpful for those beginning to study phonetics. A basic understanding of speech production provides the necessary background for production of each phoneme. Keep in mind that this chapter provides a *brief* review.

The study of phonetics that describes the physiological properties of speech is called *physiological phonetics.* Various speech organs, such as the tongue, lips, teeth, and soft palate, can be positioned to create a wide variety of speech sounds simply by making small adjustments in the move-ments and locations of the speech organs within the oral cavity. These movements are performed automatically in the accomplished speaker, and may become extremely complex in form.

The primary purpose of the structures used for speech is survival. For example, the lungs are the source of respiration, but they also provide a breath stream for speech. The tongue helps move the bolus of food to the posterior portion of the mouth so that the food can be swallowed, but it also produces speech sounds. The body parts used for speech production can be considered a

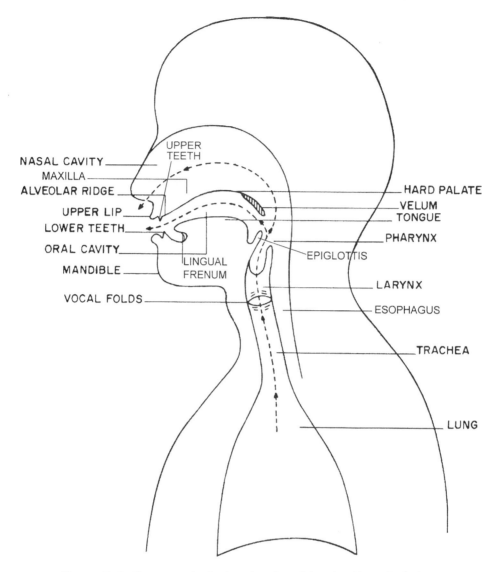

Figure 3–1. Structures in the head and neck involved in articulation.

speech-producing mechanism. Refer to Figure 3–1 and Figure 3–2 for an illustration of these body parts.

Larynx: The larynx is located in the throat, just above the trachea. It extends to the top of the esophagus, which is below the root of the tongue. Housed in the larynx are the *vocal folds*. The space between the vocal folds is the *glottis*. When the vocal folds **adduct**, or *close*, they vibrate to provide voicing for speech. When the folds **abduct**, or *open*, they

do not vibrate and voicing is not produced. Refer to Figure 3–3 for an illustration of the vocal folds.

Pharynx: This is a tubular, funnel-shaped structure located posterior to the root of the tongue and extending downward to the esophagus. The pharynx is divided into three parts: the nasopharynx, oropharynx, and the laryngopharynx (see Figure 3–2).

Nasopharynx: This is a section of the pharynx that lies directly posterior to

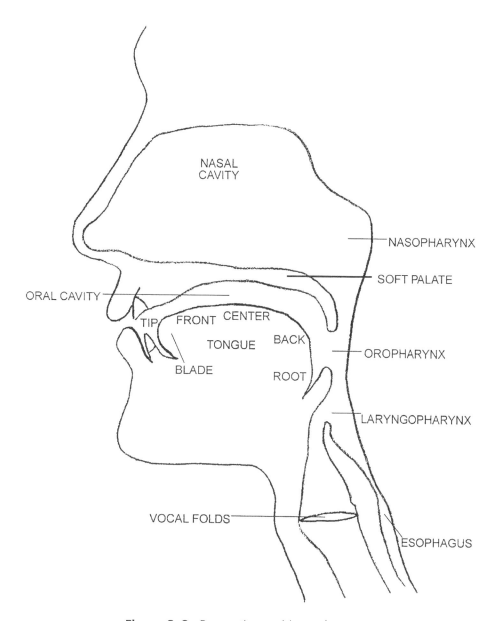

Figure 3–2. Resonating cavities and tongue.

the nasal cavity, and extends anteriorly from the nostrils to the posterior wall of the pharynx.

Oropharynx: This is a section of the pharynx that is directly posterior to the oral cavity and extends from the level of the velum above to the level of the root of the tongue below. It can be easily viewed when the mouth is wide open and the tongue is pulled forward.

Laryngopharynx: This is the lower part of the pharynx that lies directly behind the laryngeal structures.

The pharynx contains two valves: the velopharyngeal valve and the epiglottal valve.

Velopharyngeal valve: This is located at the juncture of the oropharynx and the nasopharynx. When this valve activates, it closes the nasopharynx and obstructs

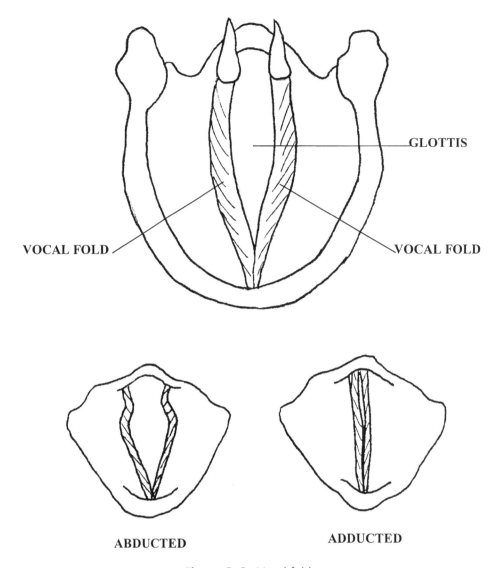

Figure 3–3. Vocal folds.

the laryngeal airstream from entering the nasopharynx and the nasal cavity.

Epiglottal valve: This is located just below the root of the tongue at the juncture of the oropharynx and the laryngopharynx. The epiglottis acts like a cover for the opening of the larynx during the passage of food from the oral cavity into the esophagus.

Oral cavity: The *oropharynx* opens anteriorly into the *oral cavity.* The oral cavity is bounded anteriorly by the lips and laterally by the cheeks. The tongue rests on the floor of the oral cavity. The hard palate and the velum form the roof of the oral cavity.

Lips: The upper and lower lips are made of muscles that have a great degree of mobility, facilitating the formation of various lip shapes for the production of vowels, such as /ɑ,o,ʊ,æ/, and consonants, such as /p,b,m,w,hw,f,v/.

Teeth: The upper and lower teeth lie posterior to the lips. The upper and lower incisors, in particular, play an important role in the production of some consonants. The consonants involving both upper and lower incisors are /θ, ð/, and the consonants involving only the upper incisors are /f, v/.

Alveolar ridge: These ridges are located in the maxilla and mandible and contain the upper and lower teeth. The area directly behind the upper anterior teeth is commonly referenced for production of lingua-alveolar consonants. It serves as the point of contact, or approximation, for the tongue tip, or front of the tongue, in the production of numerous speech sounds, such as the /t, d, l, s, z/.

Hard palate: The anterior two-thirds of the roof of the mouth is arched and comprises the bony *hard palate*. The hard palate serves as the point of contact, or the point of approximation, for the front of the tongue in the production of speech sounds, such as /ʃ, ʒ, j/.

Velum: This is the posterior one-third of the palate. It is soft and muscular. It is also known as the soft palate. The velum serves as the point of contact for the back of the tongue in the production of speech sounds such as /k, g, ŋ/. The velum, aided somewhat by the posterior pharyngeal wall musculature, forms a valve known as the *velopharyngeal valve.*

This valve opens and closes the port between the nasopharynx and the oropharynx. When the valve is open, the speech sounds produced have a nasal resonance caused by the passage of a portion of the laryngeal airstream through the nasal cavity, as in the production of English consonants /m, n, ŋ/. However, the valve is usually closed during the production of speech sounds that do not require nasal resonance, as in the production of English vowels and nonnasal consonants.

Tongue: Derived from the Latin word *"lingua,"* the tongue is an exclusively muscular organ that rests on the floor of the oral cavity. It is an extremely mobile organ capable of making innumerable changes in positioning and muscle tension guided by the action of the intrinsic (originating inside the tongue) and extrinsic (originating outside the tongue) muscles. All vowels are influenced by tongue position. The only consonants that do not have direct tongue involvement are /m, p, b, f, v/.

Lingual frenum: This is a small, white cord of tissue. This tissue extends from the floor of the oral cavity to the midline of the under surface of the tongue blade. A frenum that is too short may restrict production of sounds that require tongue elevation.

Maxilla: This is the upper jaw that forms the majority of the palate.

Mandible: This is the lower jaw. It helps to move the lower teeth close to or away from the upper teeth. Its movement helps to reduce or enlarge the size of the oral cavity. The maximum downward movement of the mandible is seen during the production of the English vowel /æ/.

Lungs: The lungs are the organ of respiration and provide a breath stream for speech. Speech is produced when the breath stream is exhaled, or expelled, from the lungs.

Trachea: These rings are composed of cartilage and membranes leading from the larynx into the lungs; often referred to as the "windpipe."

Speech Processes

Speech is the end product of the four processes of Phonation, Articulation, Respiration, and Resonance (PARR).

Phonation is accomplished with the rhythmic and rapid opening and closing of the vocal folds, which open or close the glottis.

Articulation is how the breath stream is modified to form speech sounds.

Respiration provides the flow of air for speech, which is exhalation.

Resonation is the process of vibrating air in a resonating cavity. The resonating cavities were discussed earlier in this chapter.

Articulatory Aspects of Consonants

The production of consonants can be described by the *place* of articulation (*where* the phoneme is produced), the *manner* of articulation (*how* the breath stream is modified as it passes through the oral cavity), and *voicing* (if the vocal folds adduct for a voiced phoneme or abduct for an unvoiced phoneme). The majority of the consonants of the IPA are *cognates*, which means the phonemes are made in the same place and in the same manner, with the only difference being in voicing.

Each phoneme in the IPA is identified by place, manner, voicing, and distinctive features. Distinctive features are discussed later in this chapter. As you review each phoneme page, you will find the phoneme described by manner, place, voicing, and distinctive features.

Place of Articulation

Figure 3–4 illustrates the oral cavity shapes for the places of articulation.

Bilabial: Sounds produced at the lips are known as *labial* sounds. The English phonemes /p/, /b/, /m/, /w/, and /hw/ are classified as bilabials because both (or *bi-*) lips are used to produce them. The upper and lower lips serve as *articulators*, which are

movable speech organs involved in the shaping of speech sounds. Only the lower lip is involved in production of /f/ and /v/.

Labiodental: The /f/ and /v/ phonemes are classified as *labio-* (meaning lip) and *-dental* (meaning teeth) as the lip and teeth produce those phonemes.

Linguadental: *Lingua-* (meaning tongue) and *-dental* (teeth) sounds are produced when the tip of the tongue is between the upper and lower teeth. These phonemes, /θ/ and /ð/, are also referred to as interdentals, reflecting the tongue tip position between the upper and lower teeth.

Alveolar: The *alveolar* ridge (see Figure 3–1) is a very important point of tongue contact in many world languages, including English. Numerous sounds are produced when the tongue tip touches the alveolar ridge. The /t/, /d/, /n/, /s/, /z/, /l/, and /r/ are classified as lingua-alveolar phonemes.

Palatal: The consonants /ʃ/, /ʒ/, /tʃ/, /dʒ/, and /j/ are produced by the body of the tongue contacting, or approximating, the posterior portion of the hard palate.

Velar: The consonants /k/, /g/, and /ŋ/ are classified as lingua-velar sounds when the back portion of the tongue contacts the velum, or soft palate.

Glottal: The /h/ phoneme is classified as a glottal because it is produced when the vocal folds partially adduct to create friction or turbulence. The tongue does not assume any specific position in the oral cavity, and may be in position to produce the sound that follows the /h/.

Table 3–1 summarizes place of articulation.

Table 3–2 summarizes place and manner.

Table 3–3 summarizes phonemes by place, manner, and voice.

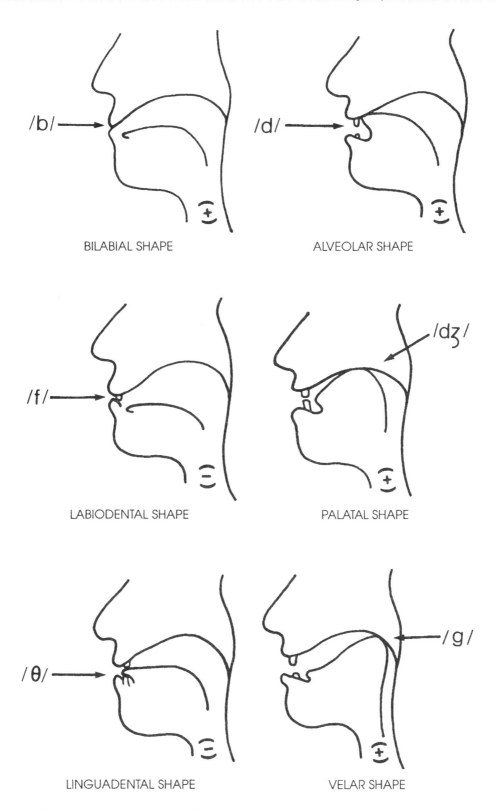

Figure 3–4. Diagram showing the six different alterations in the oral cavity shape controlled by lip and tongue contacts at the six different places along the horizontal line of the oral cavity. Plus sign (+) indicates the presence of voicing, and the minus (–) sign indicates absence of voicing.

Table 3–1. Places of Articulation

Consonant	Place of Articulation	Articulators
/p, b, m, w/	Bilabial	Lips
/f, v/	Labiodental	Lower lip and upper teeth
/θ, ð/	Linguadental	Tip of tongue and teeth
/t, d, n, s, z, l, r/	Alveolar	Tip of tongue and alveolar ridge
/ʃ, ʒ, tʃ, dʒ, j/	Palatal	Body of tongue and hard palate
/k, g, ŋ/	Velar	Back of tongue and soft palate
/h/	Glottal	Adduction/abduction of vocal folds
/hw/	Labial-Velar	Rounded lips with back of tongue approximating the soft palate

Table 3–2. Consonants Arranged by Place and Manner

Manner: →						
Place: ↓	Stop/Plosive	Fricative	Nasal	Affricate	Glides	Liquids
Bilabial	/p/(–), /b/(+)		/m/(+)		/w/(+)	
Lingua-Alveolar	/t/(–), /d/(+)	/s/(–), /z/(+)	/n/(+)			/l/(+)
Lingua-Velar	/k/(–), /g/(+)		/ŋ/(+)			
Labio-Dental		/f/(–), /v/(+)				
Interdental		/θ/(–), /ð/(+)				
Glottal		/h/(–)				
Labial-Velar		/hw/(–)				
Lingua-Palatal		/ʃ/(–), /ʒ/(+)			/j/(+)	
Alveopalatal				/tʃ/(–), /dʒ/(+)		/r/(+)

(+) Indicates a voiced phoneme.
(–) Indicates an unvoiced phoneme.

Table 3–3. IPA Phonemes Categorized by Manner, Place, and Voice

Phoneme	Manner	Place	Voicing	Comments
/p/	Stop-Consonant	Bilabial	Voiceless	Cognate of /b/
/b/	Stop-Consonant	Bilabial	Voiced	Cognate of /p/
/t/	Stop-Consonant	Lingua-Alveolar	Voiceless	Cognate of /d/
/d/	Stop-Consonant	Lingua-Alveolar	Voiced	Cognate of /t/
/k/	Stop-Consonant	Lingua-Velar	Voiceless	Cognate of /g/
/g/	Stop-Consonant	Lingua-Velar	Voiced	Cognate of /k/
/m/	Nasal	Bilabial	Voiced	Homorganic with /p/b/
/n/	Nasal	Lingua-Alveolar	Voiced	Homorganic with /t/d/
/ŋ/	Nasal	Lingua-Velar	Voiced	Homorganic with /k/g/
/f/	Fricative	Labio-Dental	Voiceless	Cognate of /v/
/v/	Fricative	Labio-Dental	Voiced	Cognate of /f/
/s/	Fricative	Lingua-Alveolar	Voiceless	Cognate of /z/
/z/	Fricative	Lingua-Alveolar	Voiced	Cognate of /s/
/θ/	Fricative	Interdental	Voiceless	Cognate of /ð/
/ð/	Fricative	Interdental	Voiced	Cognate of /θ/
/h/	Fricative	Glottal	Voiceless	—
/hw/ /ʍ/	Fricative	Labial-Velar	Voiceless	Known as inverted "w"
/ʃ/	Fricative	Lingua-Palatal	Voiceless	Cognate of /ʒ/
/ʒ/	Fricative	Lingua-Palatal	Voiced	Cognate of /ʃ/
/tʃ/	Affricate	Alveopalatal	Voiceless	Cognate of /dʒ/
/dʒ/	Affricate	Alveopalatal	Voiced	Cognate of /tʃ/
/w/	Glide	Bilabial (lingua-velar)	Voiced	—
/j/	On-Glide	Lingua-Palatal	Voiced	—
/l/	Lateral Liquid	Lingua-Alveolar	Voiced	—
/r/	Liquid (Glide)	Alveopalatal	Voiced	—
/i/	Vowel (unrounded)	High front tense	Voiced	Known as "long e"
/ɪ/	Vowel (unrounded)	High front lax	Voiced	Known as "short i"
/ɛ/	Vowel (unrounded)	Midfront lax	Voiced	Known as "short e," Epsilon
/e/	Vowel (unrounded)	Midfront tense	Voiced	Known as "long a"

continues

Table 3–3. *continued*

Phoneme	Manner	Place	Voicing	Comments
/æ/	Vowel (unrounded)	Low front lax	Voiced	Known as "short a," Ash
/ə/	Vowel (unrounded)	Midcentral lax, unstressed	Voiced	Known as the schwa
/ʌ/	Vowel (unrounded)	Midcentral, stressed	Voiced	Caret, inverted "v"
/ɚ/	R-Colored vowel	Midcentral lax, unstressed	Voiced	Hooked schwar, unstressed schwar
/ɝ/	R-Colored vowel	Midcentral tense, stressed	Voiced	Reversed hooked Epsilon
/u/	Vowel (rounded)	High back tense	Voiced	Rarely in Initial position
/ʊ/	Vowel (rounded)	High back lax	Voiced	Upsilon, capped "u"
/o/	Vowel (rounded)	Mid back tense	Voiced	Also written as /oʊ/
/ɔ/	Vowel (rounded)	Low midback lax	Voiced	Open "o" or reversed "c"
/ɑ/	Vowel (unrounded)	Low back lax	Voiced	—
/aɪ/	Diphthong (off-glide)	Rising low front to high front	Voiced	Known as "long i"
/aʊ/	Diphthong (off-glide)	Rising low front to high back	Voiced	—
/ɔɪ/	Diphthong (off-glide)	Rising mid-back to high front	Voiced	—
/ju/	Diphthong (on-glide)	High front to high back	Voiced	—

Manner of Articulation

Manner of articulation describes *how* speech sounds are produced. The articulators are positioned, and must react in a specific way, in order to produce the phoneme. The ways in which consonants are produced are described by the terms in Figure 3–5. Looking at this figure, you will note that a consonant can belong to more than one category.

See Exercises 3–A through 3–E for practice identifying manner of articulation.

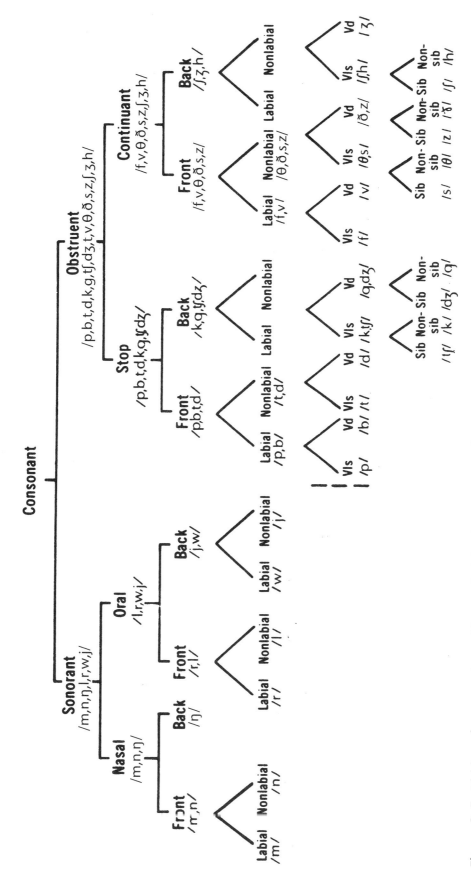

Figure 3–5. Division of consonants, on binary principles, into sonorant/obstruent, nasal/oral, stop/continuant, front/back, labial/nonlabial, voiceless/voiced (V's/Vd), and sibilant/nonsibilant (Sib/Non-Sib) groups. Reproduced with permission from *Phonetics: Principles and Practices* (3rd ed. p. 63), by S. Singh and K. Singh, 2006, Copyright 2006 Plural Publishing, Inc.

Exercises 3–A through 3–E give you an opportunity to identify manner of articulation. Circle the consonant(s) in each song title. All of these songs were recorded and/or written by the Beatles. Answers in Appendix B.

Exercise 3–A. Manner of articulation: *Stop-Consonants*

B, D, K, G
+, P

1. "Blackbird"
2. "Day Tripper"
3. "Get Back"
4. "Paperback Writer"
5. "Ticket to Ride"
6. "A Hard Day's Night"
7. "I Got to Find My Baby"
8. "I'll Be Back"
9. "Come and Get It"
10. "Let It Be"

Exercise 3–B. Manner of articulation: *Nasals*

1. "If I Needed Someone"
2. "Lady Madonna"
3. "Lend Me Your Comb"
4. "Maggie Mae"
5. "Penny Lane"
6. "Sun King"
7. "Taxman"
8. "Honeymoon Song"
9. "Tip of My Tongue"
10. "Mailman, Bring Me No More Blues"

m, n, ŋ

Exercise 3–C. Manner of articulation: *Fricatives*

F, V, θ
ð ʃ
Z ʒ
ʒ h

1. "Another Girl"
2. "Strawberry Fields Forever"
3. "Dizzy Miss Lizzy"
4. "Good Day Sunshine"
5. "Here Comes the Sun"

6. "I Saw Her Standing There"
7. "If I Fell"
8. "I've Just Seen a Face"
9. "Lucy in the Sky with Diamonds"
10. "She Came in Through the Bathroom Window"

Exercise 3–D. Manner of articulation: *Liquids and Glides*

L, R, J, W

1. "Eleanor Rigby"
2. "Lovely Rita"
3. "Yellow Submarine"
4. "Words of Love"
5. "Young Blood"
6. "Ballad of John and Yoko"
7. "Watching Rainbows"
8. "Winston's Walk"
9. "Yesterday"
10. "Run for Your Life"

Exercise 3–E. Manner of articulation: *Affricates*

+ʃ
dʒ

1. "Act Naturally"
2. "Julia"
3. "Magical Mystery Tour"
4. "Mother Nature's Son"
5. "Norwegian Wood"
6. "Blue Jay Way"
7. "Baby You're a Rich Man"
8. "Chains"
9. "Her Majesty"
10. "Hey Jude"

Obstruents: Obstruents are produced with an *obstru*ction in the vocal tract, which can be a complete or incomplete obstruction.

Sonorants: A sonorant is the opposite of an obstruent because the sound passes through a relatively open channel and is not blocked.

Stops: These phonemes are produced with a total blockage of the airstream. In these consonants, the airstream must be released after it is blocked. This class of consonants is also referred to as plosives.

Continuants: Unlike the stops, continuants are produced in a *continu*ing manner, with relatively less obstruction. Contrast production of the /t/, as in "tuh, tuh, tuh," with the continuous flow of air when producing the /s/, as in "s-s-s-s-s."

Fricatives: These phonemes are obstruents because they are produced with a partial blockage of the airstream, resulting in turbulence or *fric*tion.

Affricates: The only affricates in the IPA, /tʃ/ and /dʒ/, begin with production of a stop-consonant and end with production of a fricative.

Orals: This category refers to resonating cavities (see Figure 3–2). The consonants in this group are produced in the resonating cavity of the vocal tract, excluding the nasal cavity and nasopharynx.

Nasals: The /m/, /n/, and /ŋ/ are the only consonants requiring nasal resonance. The resonating cavity is the entire vocal tract, including the nasal cavity and the nasopharynx. Nasal resonance is accomplished by the lowering of the velum to permit airflow into the nasal cavity.

Liquids and glides: The consonants /r/, /l/, /w/, and /j/ are considered liquids and glides because of their extreme flexibility in assuming the role of either a consonant or a vowel. The /l/ is also called a lateral because it is the only phoneme with airflow around the *sides* of the tongue.

Voiced and voiceless: This category focuses on the vibration of the vocal folds. In a voiced phoneme, the vocal folds are *add*ucted and vibrate. In voiceless sounds, the vocal folds are *ab*ducted and no voicing is produced.

Articulatory Aspects of Vowels

Vowel classification differs greatly from the system used to classify consonants. Vowels are classified by tongue position. All vowels require voicing produced by the vibrating vocal folds. Refer to Chapter 9 for more information about vowels.

Distinctive Features

Distinctive features are those attributes of a phoneme that are required to differentiate one phoneme from another in a language. For example, the phonemes /k/ and /g/ in English are differentiated by the feature of voicing, which in turn is an attribute in differentiating phonemes in the English language. Figure 3–6 displays distinctive feature contrast for English consonants.

The features are:

Voicing/voiceless: The vocal folds *add*uct for a voiced phoneme and *ab*duct for a voiceless phoneme.

Front/back: The consonant is produced in the front of the vocal tract (lips, alveolar ridge), or in the back of the vocal tract (hard or soft palate).

Labial/nonlabial: One or both lips are used in producing the consonant or the lips are not used to form the sound.

Sonorant/nonsonorant: The relatively open vocal tract is used to produce a sonorant consonant; nonsonorant refers to an obstructed vocal tract.

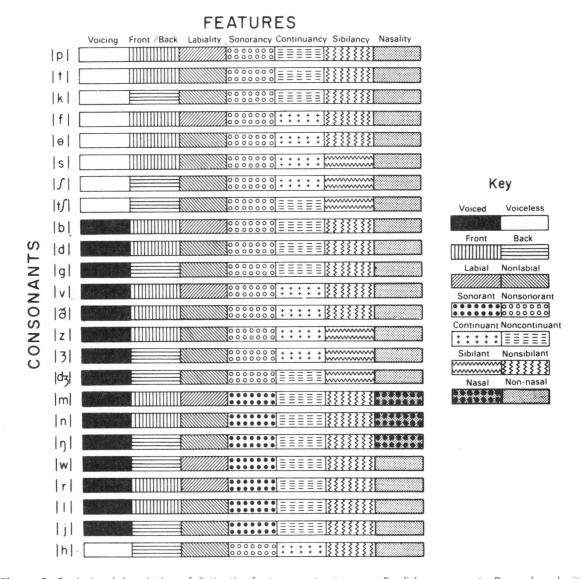

Figure 3–6. A visual description of distinctive feature contrast among English consonants. Reproduced with permission from *Phonetics: Principles and Practices* (3rd ed. p. 168), by S. Singh and K. Singh, 2006, Copyright 2006 Plural Publishing, Inc.

Continuant/noncontinuant: Continuant phonemes are made without a constriction so that the airflow is not blocked. A noncontinuant sound is constricted.

Sibilant/nonsibilant: Consonants with this distinctive feature have a "hissing" sound, such as the /s/ or /ʃ/.

Nasal/non-nasal: Nasal consonants require nasal resonance through lowering of the velopharyngeal port to allow the airflow into the nasal cavity.

Ages of Consonant Development

Table 3–4 presents data summarized from several studies indicating ages of consonant development. You will note variation in age of acquisition of the various consonants.

Table 3–4. Developmental Norms for Phonemes

Phonemes	Wellman et al. (1931)	Poole (1934)	Templin (1957)	Sander (1972)	Prather et al. (1975)	Arlt et al. (1976)	Fudala & Reynolds (1986)	Smit et al. (1990)
m	3	3½	3	≤2	2	3	2 ½	≤3½
n	3	4½	3	≤2	2	3	2	≤3½
h	3	3½	3	≤2	2	3	1½	≤3
p	4	3½	3	≤2	2	3	2	3 to 3½
f	3	5½	3	3	2 to 4	3	2 ½	3½ to 4
w	3	3½	3	≤2	2 to 8	3	1½	≤3
b	3	3½	4	≤2	2 to 8	3	2	≤3
ŋ	—	4½	3	2	2	3	—	≥9
j	4	4½	3½	3½	3	3	3	3½ to 4
k	4	4½	4	2	2 to 4	3	2½	≤4
g	4	4½	4	2	2 to 4	3	2½	3 to 4
l	4	6½	6	3	2 to 4	4	5	5 to 6
d	5	4½	4	2	2 to 4	3	2½	≤3½
t	5	4½	6	2	2 to 8	3	3	≤3½
s	5	7½	4½	3	3	4	11	9
r	5	7½	4	3	3 to 4	5	5½	8
tʃ	5	—	4½	4	3 to 8	4	5½	5½ to 7
v	5	6½	6	4	4+	3½	5½	4½ to 5½
z	5	7½	7	4	4+	4	11	≥ 9
ʒ	6	6½	7	6	4	4	—	—
θ	—	7½	6	5	4+	5	5½	6 to 7
dʒ	—	—	7	4	4+	4	5	6 to 7
ʃ	—	6½	4	4	3 to 8	4½	5½	6 to 7
ð	—	6½	7	5	4	5	5½	4½ to 7

Source: Reproduced with permission from *Assessment of Communication Disorders in Children* (2nd ed.), by M. N. Hegde and F. Pomaville, 2013, p. 153. Copyright 2013 by Plural Publishing, Inc.

Consonant Clusters

A *consonant cluster*, also referred to as a *consonant blend*, is a combination of two or more adjacent consonants in the same syllable. The words "tree" [tri] and "street" [strit] have double and triple consonant clusters, respectively, in the initial position of the word. Clusters can also occur in the medial position (underlined) as in "restrain" [ri<u>str</u>en] or in the final position as in "fast" [fæ<u>st</u>].

A consonant cluster is simply a way of combining the consonant phonemes in a language. Only certain consonants can be used to form clusters. Although initial consonant clusters /st/, /sk/, /sp/, and /sw/ occur in English, clusters such as /sb/, /sd/, /sg/, /sr/, and /sv/ are not found in the initial position of a word in English. Table 3–5 provides numerous examples of clusters in Standard American English in the initial (syllable-initiating) and final (syllable-terminating) positions.

Table 3–5. Examples of Consonant Clusters in American English

Consonant Cluster	Word Examples	Consonant Cluster	Word Examples
Syllable Initiating (Initial)		**Syllable Terminating (Final)**	
bl-	bleak, blame, black	-ft	left, lift, soft
fl-	flake, flag, flee	-gz	wigs, rags, bugs
gl-	glad, glow, gleam	-ks	lacks, walks, likes
kl-	clean, clap, close	-kt	pact, fact, act
pl-	plan, pleat, plow		
sl-	sleep, slide, slender	-lb	bulb
		-ld	mold, bald, sold
br-	brain, bring, brag	-lf	elf, calf, shelf
dr-	dress, drink, drip	-lk	walk, elk, milk
fr-	frame, frost, fright	-lp	help, gulp, pulp
gr-	grin, grape, grip	-lt	salt, fault, malt
kr-	cry, creep, crop	-lz	sells, malls, wheels
pr-	price, practical, pro		
tr-	trim, treat, trick	-mp	stamp, jump, bump
shr-	shred, shrub, shrine	-mpt	stomped, jumped, bumped
thr-	through, threat, throw	-mps	lamps, ramps, jumps
		-mz	arms, stems, aims
sk-	scoop, schedule, skim		
skr-	scream, screech, scrap	-nd	hand, bend, wind
skw-	squeal, squash, squander	-ndz	hands, bends, grounds
		-nt	ant, rent, print
sm-	smile, smear, smug	-nts	prints, joints, ants
		-nz	plans, runs, burns
sn-	sneak, snow, sniff		
		-ŋk	junk, sank, bank
sp-	speak, spot, sparkle	-ŋz	kings, wings, sings
spl-	splash, splendor, split		
spr-	sprout, spring, spruce	-pt	roped, seeped, shopped
st-	stew, stop, steel	-rd	guard, sword, hard
str-	strike, street, stripe	-rf	scarf
		-rk	fork, shark, mark
kw-	queen, quantity, quiver	-rm	charm, form, dorm
		-rn	learn, fern, barn
sw-	sweet, swipe, swat	-rst	first, worst, burst
tw-	twin, twenty, tweezer	-rt	cart, sort, art
fj-	few, future, fume	-rv	carve, starve, nerve
kj-	cute, cube, accuse	-st	nest, past, test
mj-	music, amuse, stimulate	-ts	mats, bets, sits

STUDY QUESTIONS

1. What is the primary purpose of the structures used for speech?

Survival

2. Define PARR.

Four processes that result in speech, phonation-articulation - respiration - resonance

3. How do place and manner of articulation differ?

Place is where the sound is produced & manner is how it is produced

4. How do nasals gain resonance?

lowering the velum, to permit air flow into the nasal cavity

5. What is the difference between adducted and abducted vocal folds?

adduct - close → vibration
abduct - open → no vibration

6. Fill in the anatomic structure associated with production of:

  a. Bilabials   lips
  b. Glottals   vocal folds
  c. Linguadentals   tongue & teeth
  d. Alveolars   alveolar ridge
  e. Palatals   tongue & hard palate
  f. Velars   tongue & soft palate

7. What is a cluster or blend?

a combination of 2 or more adjacent consonants in the same syllable   ex: fast, street

8. What is the difference between an obstruent and a sonorant?

An obstruent has a considerable amount of obstruction, meanwhile a sonorant requires a negligible amount.

CHAPTER

4

Stop-Consonants

Learning Objectives

After reading this chapter, you will be able to:

1. Explain the two phases of production of a stop-consonant.

2. Define a glottal stop and voiced /t/, and the difference in place and manner of production.

3. Identify cognates of /p/t/k/.

4. Transcribe words using stop-consonants.

Stop-consonants, also known as plosives, require a stopping of the breath stream by a closure within the oral cavity. Production of a stop-consonant is a *manner* of articulation. Manner of articulation is discussed in Chapter 3. There are two phases involved in production of a stop-consonant: the air must be stopped and then it must be released. Stopping of the air is mandatory, as air must be held in the oral cavity. The plosive phase of the stop releases the impounded air. Stopping of the airstream can occur by lip closure, as in producing /b/, tongue elevation, as in production of /t/, or by adduction of the vocal folds for a glottal stop.

Release of the air, also known as aspiration, can occur in two ways. The air can be released as a "puff" of air, similar to that of

an ex*plosion*, when released into a vowel, as in the word "pay" [pʰe] or released without the explosion of air, as in the phrase "*at* work." The symbol [ʰ] identifies aspiration of the impounded air, and the [˺] denotes unreleased air.

Edwards (2003) discusses "The Strange Case of the American English /t/" and lists ten allophonic variations. An allophonic variation is a difference in the way a phoneme can be produced. The /t/ does differ from other English consonants because of its many variations. For example, the /t/ may be voiced, substituted with a glottal stop, or intruded in a word. The following are transcription exercises for some of these variations in this chapter.

/p/

Transcription Exercise 4–1

🔊)) **AUDIO 1–5**

		I	M	F
1.	phone			
2.	split			
3.	hiccough			
4.	gopher			
5.	shopping			
6.	president			
7.	peppermint			
8.	pneumatic			
9.	append			
10.	pamphlet			

Transcription Exercise 4–2

🔊 **AUDIO 1–6**

Consonant: /p/

Refer to Study Card: 3

Phonetic Symbol	Target Word	Transcription
/p/	1. pine	paɪn
	2. deep	dip
	3. oppose	əpoʊz
	4. cape	keɪp
	5. paper	peɪpɚ
	6. sip	sɪp
	7. place	pleɪs
	8. help	hɛlp
	9. pack	pæk

/p/

Distinctive Features	Tongue Position
Bilabial stop-consonant Voiceless, front, labial, nonsonorant, noncontinuant, nonsibilant, nonnasal 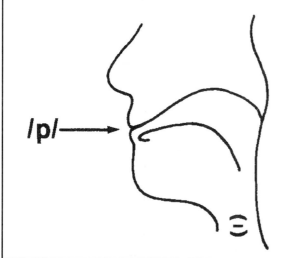	Not relevant for production of this phoneme. May be in position for following consonant or vowel. Lips are closed. Breath is held and compressed in oral cavity. Breath stream may or may not be released with aspiration; dependent upon surrounding consonants and syllable position.

Voicing/Velopharyngeal Port	Spelling Variations

Voiceless—vocal folds *ab*duct.
 	
VP port is closed.
	Appears as /p/ in words
	
	Appears in clusters with /l/r/s/spl/spr/
	
	pp in medial position (a*pp*ly/o*pp*ose) is transcribed with a single /p/.
	
	This phoneme may be intruded in the following words if an unvoiced phoneme follows a nasal:
	
	    warmth [wormpθ]
	
	    comfort [kʌmpfɚt]
	
	    dreamt [drɛmpt].

Word Position	Clinical Information
Initial, medial, and final positions in SAE	Cognate of /b/

/b/

Transcription Exercise 4–3

		I	M	F
1.	humble			
2.	ribbon			
3.	belabor			
4.	public			
5.	Burbank			
6.	thumb			
7.	probe			
8.	halibut			
9.	broke			
10.	tombstone			

Transcription Exercise 4–4

Consonant: /b/

🔊 AUDIO 1–8

Refer to Study Card: 4

Phonetic Symbol	Target Word	Transcription
/b/	1. bad	bæd
	2. tub	tʌb
	3. baby	beɪbi
	4. bright	brəɪt
	5. rabbit	ræbət
	6. nobody	noʊbadi
	7. bomb	bam
	8. cob	kab
	9. curb	kɝb

/b/

Distinctive Features	Tongue Position
Bilabial stop-consonant Voiced, front, labial, nonsonorant, noncontinuant, nonsibilant, nonnasal /b/ →	Irrelevant; tongue may be in position for following consonant or vowel. Lips are closed. Breath is held and compressed in oral cavity. Breath stream may or may not be released with aspiration; dependent upon surrounding consonants and syllable position.

Voicing/Velopharyngeal Port	Spelling Variations
Voiced—Vocal folds *ad*duct. VP port is closed.	bb in medial position (ho*bb*y, ru*bb*er) is transcribed with a single /b/ pb occurs rarely as /b/ in cu*pb*oard silent /b/ in bom*b*.

Word Positions	Clinical Information
Initial, medial, and final positions in SAE	Cognate of /p/

Crossword Puzzle for /p/ and /b/

Answers in Appendix B

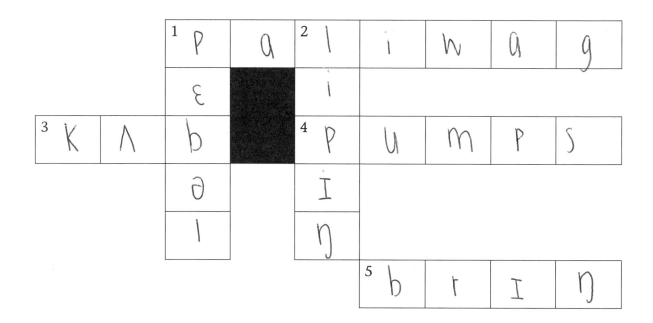

Directions: Transcribe the following words:

Across:

1. pollywog
3. cub
4. pumps
5. bring

Down:

1. pebble
2. leaping

4. PΛMPS
      ☆ wrote u by accident

BABYTIME

Word Search #1   Answers in Appendix B

s	ʃ	r	d	aɪ	p	ɚ	z	b	ɔ	l	t	z	r
d	ʒ	ɚ	k	ʃ	ə	b	p	æ	n	d	ə	ð	ʌ
b	ɑ	t	ə	l	o	r	r	i	æ	k	n	ʊ	d
s	tʃ	i	w	b	l	u	p	m	ɪ	p	z	n	ʍ
h	p	ɛ	t	e	v	i	b	b	e	u	l	m	p
f	ɑ	ʒ	ŋ	b	ɛ	ʌ	ɔ	k	r	ɪ	p	t	s
k	p	t	θ	i	p	z	z	t	dʒ	i	b	v	n
l	ɑ	s	l	z	ð	w	k	m	æ	ʒ	n	æ	p
b	ɛ	f	o	ɪ	ɛ	r	ʃ	ɪ	k	o	u	r	æ
h	b	æ	s	ɪ	n	ɛ	t	r	g	l	ʊ	f	s
n	ɪ	z	ɛ	g	ɔ	ɪ	ʌ	i	d	r	s	n	ɪ
s	b	e	b	ɪ	b	n	z	b	ʌ	n	i	g	f
p	ɪ	ŋ	k	w	dʒ	ð	b	e	ʌ	ɛ	ɪ	ʒ	aɪ
j	f	e	ɪ	w	ə	p	r	w	ɝ	g	v	z	j
l	b	l	æ	ŋ	k	ɛ	t	p	t	d	i	ɔ	ɚ
r	g	h	p	ks	f	m	ɚ	b	g	ɑ	r	ə	g

Directions: Find and circle the words listed below that contain the /p/ or /b/ phonemes.

papa	pacifier	bunny	bassinet
panda	bib	diapers	blanket
pink	bottle	blue	nap
baby			

(handwritten)
papa →
panda →
pink →
baby →
pacifier →
bib →
bottle →
bunny →
diapers →
blue →
bassinet →
blanket →
nap →

/t/

Transcription Exercise 4–5

◀)) AUDIO 1–9

		I	M	F
1.	caught			
2.	whistle			
3.	tuition			
4.	thyme			
5.	tentative			
6.	tortilla			
7.	watched			
8.	chalet			
9.	territory			
10.	motion			

Transcription Exercise 4–6

🔊 **AUDIO 1–10**

Consonant: /t/

Refer to Study Card: 5

Phonetic Symbol	Target Word	Transcription
/t/	1. tube	
	2. cut	
	3. into	
	4. until	
	5. twin	
	6. coat	
	7. rotate	
	8. time	
	9. nest	

/t/

Distinctive Features	Tongue Position
Lingua-alveolar stop-consonant Voiceless, front, nonlabial, nonsonorant, noncontinuant, nonsibilant, nonnasal /t/ ⟶	Tip of tongue contacts alveolar ridge with sides against upper molars. Breath is held in oral cavity; may be released with or without aspiration.

Voicing/Velopharyngeal Port	Spelling Variations
Voiceless—vocal folds *ab*duct VP port is closed.	Usually occurs as /t/ tt transcribed as a single /t/ in medial position as in li*tt*le -ed following unvoiced consonants as in wish*ed*, cough*ed*, tap*ed* is transcribed with a /t/, except following the /t/ as in skat*ed* or wait*ed*. th as in *Th*omas, *Th*eresa transcribed as /t/ n( )s results in an intruded /t/ sound, not included in spelling, between /n/ and /s/ as in chance [tʃænᵗs] or tense [tɛnᵗs]. t is silent in sof*t*en, cas*t*le, whis*t*le.

Word Position	Clinical Information
Initial, medial, and final positions in SAE	Commonly replaced with the voiced /t/ or glottal stop Cognate of /d/ tr- in *tr*anquil or *tr*actor can be produced as the /tʃ/.

The Glottal Stop

Transcription Exercise 4–7   🔊 **AUDIO 1–11**

Remember these things about the glottal stop:

1 It is an allophonic variation of the /t/ and /k/.

2 Do not confuse the glottal stop with a question mark. It is written as "ʔ"

3 When followed by an "n" in the spelling of the word, a syllabic /n̩/ is used.

The glottal stop is produced by the vocal folds when they *ad*duct to hold air in the glottis (space between the vocal folds) and *ab*duct to release the air. This exercise will give you an opportunity to hear the difference between production of the /t/ and the glottal stop.

Word	/t/ transcription	Glottal stop transcription
1. Doolittle		
2. mitten		
3. fountain		
4. patent		
5. Hilton		
6. button		
7. Latin		
8. cotton		
9. bitten		
10. molten		

The Voiced /t/

Transcription Exercise 4–8    AUDIO 1–12

Like the glottal stop, the voiced /t/ is an allophonic variation of the /t/. It is an alternative pronunciation. The voiced /t/ can result when voiced phonemes precede and follow the /t/. In the examples that follow (with the exception of #3, "battle"), the /t/ is *intervocalic* (between two vowels), and the voiced sounds that surround the /t/ cause it to be voiced.

Voicing of the /t/ is dependent on syllable stress (Chapter 14). If the second syllable containing the /t/ is not stressed, this allows for voicing of the /t/. Example: "total" could be transcribed as ['toṭəl]. If the word is produced with stress on the second syllable containing the /t/, then the word is transcribed as [to'təl]. Pronounce these words: *detain*, *enter*, and *control*. These are examples of words with second syllable stress in which the /t/ would not be voiced.

Accurate transcription is required to clarify what word the speaker has produced. For example, did the speaker say "bidder" [bɪdɚ] or "bitter" [bɪṭɚ]? Narrow transcription of the /t/ is required to clarify which word was said for accurate transcription.

Transcribe the following words. Words in the first column are dictated with the /t/. The second column words are dictated with the voiced /t/. Remember that the voiced /t/ sounds like the /d/. Here is a rule for using a voiced /t/: *If a word is spelled with a "t," but you hear a "d," use the "v" (for voicing) /ṭ/.*

Word	/t/ transcription	Voiced /t/ transcription
1. better	_____	_____
2. hotter	_____	_____
3. battle	_____	_____
4. matter	_____	_____
5. atom	_____	_____
6. butter	_____	_____
7. cater	_____	_____
8. quota	_____	_____
9. cheated	_____	_____
10. duty	_____	_____

Some phoneticians use the alveolar flap, (or tap), /ɾ/ to transcribe the voiced /t/. The term describes the tongue tip and blade briefly contacting, or flapping, against the upper alveolar ridge. Unlike production of the /t/, there is no buildup of air pressure. Shriberg and Kent (2012) describe the flap as a "modified stop." Edwards (2003) states the intervocalic /t/ can be transcribed as /ţ/ or /ɾ/. It is very difficult to *hear* the difference between a voiced /ţ/ or flap when words are produced. Ladefoged (2005) provides a detailed discussion of the alveolar flap. Test your listening skills: Listen to Elvis Presley sing "In the Ghetto" (Mac Davis, 1969). Do you hear Elvis sing the word as ['gɛţo] or [gɛ'to]?

/d/

Transcription Exercise 4–9

 AUDIO 1–13

		I	M	F
1.	hedge			
2.	handkerchief			
3.	mapped			
4.	deadened			
5.	decade			
6.	pointed			
7.	adding			
8.	medial			
9.	dread			
10.	demand			

Transcription Exercise 4–10

Consonant: /d/

◀)) **AUDIO 1–14**

Refer to Study Card: 6

Phonetic Symbol	Target Word	Transcription
/d/	1. dough	
	2. condition	
	3. used	
	4. dish	
	5. meadow	
	6. sand	
	7. dwell	
	8. wonder	
	9. changed	

/d/

Distinctive Features	Tongue Position
Lingua-alveolar stop-consonant Voiced front, nonlabial, nonsonorant, noncontinuant, nonsibilant, non-nasal /d/ ⟶	Same as for the cognate /t/ As a voiced phoneme, less breath pressure is required than for voiceless /t/.

Voicing/Velopharyngeal Port	Spelling Variations
Voiced—vocal folds *ad*duct. VP port is closed.	d is primary. dd is transcribed with a /d/ as in a*dd* or sa*dd*er. -ed has sound of /d/ following vowels as in mow*ed* and pray*ed* and voiced consonants, as in sav*ed* or open*ed*. ld occurs with silent /l/ in cou*ld*, shou*ld*.

Word Position	Clinical Information
Initial, medial, and final positions in SAE	Cognate of /t/ dr- in *dr*ive or *dr*ink can be produced as the /dʒ/.

Crossword Puzzle for /t/ and /d/

Answer in Appendix B

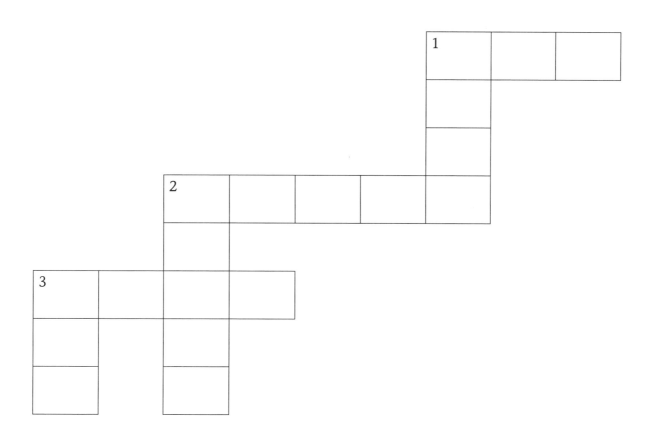

Directions: Transcribe the following words:

Across:

1. deaf
2. disease
3. data

Down:

1. dimes
2. detour
3. dot

/k/

Transcription Exercise 4–11

 AUDIO 1–15

		I	M	F
1.	centimeter			
2.	pique			
3.	quartet			
4.	text			
5.	bronchitis			
6.	impeccable			
7.	critic			
8.	backache			
9.	knight			
10.	Tocqueville			

Transcription Exercise 4–12

 **AUDIO 1–16**

Consonant: /k/

Refer to Study Card: 1

Phonetic Symbol	Target Word	Transcription
/k/	1. back	
	2. count	
	3. tick	
	4. basket	
	5. cake	
	6. cream	
	7. stocking	
	8. across	
	9. marquee	

/k/

Distinctive Features	Tongue Position
Lingua-velar stop-consonant Voiceless, back, nonlabial, nonsonorant, noncontinuant, nonsibilant, non-nasal 	Back of tongue elevates to touch velum. Air pressure builds up behind tongue/velum seal. Lips are apart and neutral. Air pressure is released when tongue moves from velum.
Voicing/Velopharyngeal Port	**Spelling Variations**
Voiceless—vocal folds *ab*duct. VP port is closed.	Numerous variations cc as in "o*cc*ur" transcribed with a single /k/. ch as in a*ch*e, *ch*orus ck always has /k/ sound as in du*ck*, ti*ck* que as in techni*que*. kh as in *kh*aki ng ( ) th results in an intruded /k/, not included in the spelling of the word, as in length [lɛŋkθ] Cluster examples: kl, kr, sk, skw, skr
Word Position	**Clinical Information**
Initial, medial, and final positions in SAE	/t/ is often substituted for /k/ in young children. Cognate of /g/

/g/

Transcription Exercise 4–13   🔊 AUDIO 1–17

		I	M	F
1.	gentle			
2.	garbage			
3.	gnat			
4.	eggnog			
5.	exist			
6.	gouge			
7.	laugh			
8.	Gertrude			
9.	linger			
10.	digit			

Transcription Exercise 4–14

🔊 AUDIO 1–18

Consonant: /g/

Refer to Study Card: 2

Phonetic Symbol	Target Word	Transcription
/g/	1. gone	
	2. wiggle	
	3. hungry	
	4. beg	
	5. dog	
	6. green	
	7. vague	
	8. glove	
	9. griddle	

/g/

Distinctive Features	Tongue Position
Lingua-velar stop-consonant Voiced back, nonlabial, nonsonorant, noncontinuant, nonsibilant, nonnasal 	Same as for /k/ Produced with less breath pressure and muscular tension than /k/

Voicing/Velopharyngeal Port	Spelling Variations
Voiced—vocal folds *ad*duct. VP port is closed.	gg transcribed with single /g/ sound Exception: su*gg*est [sʌgdʒɛst] *gu*e as in vo*gue* *gu* as in *gu*est, *gu*ard *gh* as in *gh*ost (e)x as in *exist* has the /gz/ sound [ɛgzɪst]

Word Positions	Clinical Information
Initial, medial, and final positions in SAE	Common articulatory substitution: d/g Cognate of /k/

Crossword Puzzle for /k/ and /g/

Answers in Appendix B

Directions: Transcribe the following words:

Across:
2. sugar
3. breakfast
5. coffee
6. napkin

Down:
1. yogurt
3. bacon
4. eggs

SPICE UP YOUR LIFE

Word Search #2   Answers in Appendix B

g	u	o	t	aɪ	m	b	k	ʌ	v	l	ɛ	k	t
k	ɔ	v	i	r	n	ʌ	t	m	ɛ	g	n	g	d
e	ʌ	d	ð	ɝ	ɝ	w	z	s	f	j	ɔ	t	ʃ
p	k	ɛ	k	i	k	ju	m	ɪ	n	h	ʒ	ɝ	o
ɚ	w	s	ɚ	ʌ	æ	ə	c	h	l	e	h	m	ɛ
z	i	o	l	t	k	f	u	d	o	ɛ	m	ɚ	ɚ
e	k	ɛ	r	o	w	e	r	ɪ	t	ð	ɪ	ɪ	ʌ
h	s	r	æ	r	k	d	k	l	p	p	o	k	θ
k	f	t	k	ɛ	ɛ	v	m	t	r	t	l	p	n
r	k	m	d	g	r	k	ɔ	r	i	æ	n	d	ɚ
g	ɝ	æ	v	ə	t	r	o	ŋ	h	ɪ	t	b	m
b	i	ð	r	n	θ	p	æ	p	r	i	k	ə	g
o	ɪ	ɛ	k	o	g	t	n	ð	e	ʒ	æ	v	r
w	n	k	l	o	v	z	h	e	v	d	ɛ	g	j
f	tʃ	z	i	u	n	t	ɛ	r	ə	g	ɑ	n	ə
k	ɑ	r	d	ə	m	ə	m	ɛ	n	æ	t	tʃ	t

Directions: Find and circle the words listed below that contain the /t/d/k/ or /g/ phonemes.

caraway	turmeric	cumin	dill
cardamom	capers	oregano	coriander
curry	paprika	nutmeg	tarragon
thyme	cloves		

Stop-Consonant

Transcription Exercise 4–15

/ p / b / t / d / k / g /

🔊 **AUDIO 1–19**

Phoneme Study Cards: 1–6

1. perpetrate   _____

2. bucket   _____

3. clay pot   _____

4. dropped   _____

5. Pope   _____

6. dot-to-dot   _____

7. cupcake   _____

8. babied   _____

9. deadbolt   _____

10. coat   _____

11. pagoda   _____

12. bird beak   _____

13. fixed   _____

14. laptop   _____

15. gabby   _____

16. dog tag   _____

17. backup   _____

18. toga   _____

19. pocketbook   _____

20. kept   _____

STUDY QUESTIONS

1. Name two phases of stop-consonant production.

   _____

   _____

2. How is a glottal stop produced?

   _____

   _____

3. How do consonant cognates differ?

   _____

   _____

4. How is the alveolar flap/tap produced?

   _____

   _____

5. What are some allophonic variations of the /t/?

   _____

   _____

6. List the cognates for these stop-consonants:

   a. /k/ _____

   b. /t/ _____

   c. /p/ _____

7. List three things to remember about production of a glottal stop (refer to Transcription Exercise 4–7).

   _____

   _____

   _____

CHAPTER

5

Consonants:
Nasals and Syllabics

Learning Objectives

After reading this chapter, you will be able to:

1. Identify place of production of the nasal consonants.

2. State the position of velopharyngeal port when a nasal is produced.

3. Define a syllabic consonant and give examples.

4. Explain the term "homorganic" and relationship to syllabic consonants.

5. List homorganic consonants for all nasals.

6. Transcribe words using nasal consonants.

Nasal Consonants

The nasal consonants are /m/n/ŋ/. They are the only consonants produced with nasal resonance. The velum is lowered, opening the velopharyngeal port to allow the breath stream to enter the nasal cavity. Each nasal consonant differs in place of production. The /m/ is a bilabial and is produced with bilabial lip closure. Tongue position is not relevant for the /m/. The /n/ is produced with lingua-alveolar contact. The /ŋ/ is formed by the back portion of the tongue contacting the velum. All of the nasals are voiced.

/m/

Transcription Exercise 5–1

 AUDIO 1–20

		I	M	F
1.	mermaid			
2.	dime			
3.	palm			
4.	mum			
5.	chasm			
6.	minimum			
7.	membrane			
8.	hammer			
9.	squirm			
10.	empire			

Transcription Exercise 5–2

🔊)) **AUDIO 1–21**

Consonant: /m/

Refer to Study Card: 19

Phonetic Symbol	Target Word	Transcription
/m/	1. might	
	2. lamp	
	3. meat	
	4. team	
	5. camera	
	6. malt	
	7. random	
	8. harm	
	9. smell	

/m/

Distinctive Features	Tongue Position
Bilabial Nasal Voiced, front, labial, sonorant, noncontinuant, nonsibilant, nasal /m/→ → open velopharyngeal port	Tongue is flat in the oral cavity or is in place for the following phoneme. Lips are closed.

Voicing/Velopharyngeal Port	Spelling Variations
Voiced—vocal folds *ad*ducted. VP port is open—airflow through nasal cavity.	mm as in su*mm*er is transcribed with a single /m/. gm with silent /g/ as in diaphra*gm* mb with silent /b/ as in nu*mb* mn with silent /n/ as in hy*mn*

Word Positions	Clinical Information
Initial, medial, and final positions in SAE	Lips are brought together as for production of the bilabials /p/ and /b/. Homorganic (made in the same place) with /p/ and /b/

/n/

Transcription Exercise 5–3   ◀)) AUDIO 1–22

		I	M	F
1.	knapsack			
2.	kennel			
3.	nonsense			
4.	zone			
5.	gnash			
6.	pneumatic			
7.	noon			
8.	gnome			
9.	beginner			
10.	seventeen			

Transcription Exercise 5–4

 **AUDIO 1–23**

Consonant: /n/

Refer to Study Card: 20

Phonetic Symbol	Target Word	Transcription
/n/	1. tennis	
	2. cabin	
	3. noisy	
	4. canary	
	5. nautical	
	6. violin	
	7. handy	
	8. panel	
	9. nylon	

/n/

Distinctive Features	Tongue Position
Lingua-alveolar nasal consonant	Tip of tongue touches the alveolar ridge.
Voiced, front, nonlabial, sonorant, noncontinuant, nonsibilant, nasal	Front of tongue touches the upper alveolar ridge.
	Sides of tongue touch upper molars.
	Back of tongue is down.
/n/ → open velopharyngeal port	Teeth and lips are open.

Voicing/Velopharyngeal Port	Spelling Variations
Voiced—vocal folds *ad*ducted.	nn as in i*nn* transcribed with a single /n/
VP port is open—airflow through nasal cavity.	mn silent /m/ as in *mn*emonic
	pn silent /p/ as in *pn*eumonia
	kn silent /k/ as in *kn*ee
	gn silent /g/ as in si*gn*

Word Positions	Clinical Information
Initial, medial, and final positions in SAE	Homorganic (made in the same place) with /t/ and /d/

TAKE TIME TO SMELL THE FLOWERS

Word Search #3

Answers in Appendix B

m	e	m	æ	g	n	o	l	j	ə	l	n
d	o	ə	p	k	d	ɝ	i	e	ɪ	z	ɛ
ɛ	f	o	r	dʒ	u	ʌ	p	ɛ	u	ŋ	r
l	r	ð	ɪ	n	n	s	i	ɪ	o	p	v
f	s	m	m	ʌ	m	t	t	u	o	æ	θ
ɪ	p	ʃ	r	j	v	ks	u	ʊ	ɝ	n	g
n	b	t	o	d	f	k	n	b	ɚ	z	o
i	t	ɪ	z	e	p	ɑ	i	i	ə	i	k
ə	d	s	o	m	ɛ	r	ə	g	o	l	d
m	k	r	p	i	o	n	i	o	ʌ	s	h
ə	g	ʊ	z	tʃ	w	e	ʒ	n	k	s	ʒ
dʒ	æ	z	m	i	n	ʃ	z	i	g	z	z
j	w	ɔ	ɪ	æ	n	ə	e	ə	s	r	v
ʌ	z	ɪ	n	i	ə	n	w	o	z	w	f

Directions: Find and circle the words listed below that contain the /m/ or /n/ phonemes.

mum	petunia	primrose
carnation	jasmine	zinnia
delphinium	magnolia	pansy
peony	begonia	marigold

/ŋ/

Transcription Exercise 5–5   🔊 **AUDIO 1–24**

		I	M	F
1.	monkey			
2.	singing			
3.	kingdom			
4.	arrange			
5.	elongate			
6.	wrong			
7.	jingle			
8.	length			
9.	fangs			
10.	sponge			

Transcription Exercise 5–6

 **AUDIO 1–25**

Consonant: /ŋ/

Refer to Study Card: 21

Reminder: Use /ɪ/ before "ing" words. See page 82.

Phonetic Symbol	Target Word	Transcription
/ŋ/	1. bongo	
	2. strongly	
	3. Hong Kong	
	4. wing	
	5. tongue	
	6. shingle	
	7. dining	
	8. fang	
	9. savings	

/ŋ/

Distinctive Features	Tongue Position
Lingua-velar nasal consonant Voiced, back, nonlabial, sonorant, noncontinuant, nonsibilant, nasal open velopharyngeal port /ŋ/	Back of tongue is raised to contact velum. Sides of back of tongue contact back molars. Teeth and lips are open. Voice is directed through open VP port to nasal cavity.

Voicing/Velopharyngeal Port	Spelling Variations
Voiced—vocal folds *ad*ducted. VP port is open—airflow through nasal cavity.	Occurs as ng in words n (k) appears in mi*nk* [mɪŋk] or si*nk*. In the same syllable and often in adjoining syllables as in i*nc*ome [ɪŋkʌm]. ng as in si*ng*le [sɪŋəl] ngue as in to*ngue* [tʌŋ]

Word Positions	Clinical Information
Medial and final positions in SAE	Homorganic (made in the same place) with /k/ and /g/ Also called the "hooked n."

Why Use The /ɪ/ Before /ŋ/?

The high front vowel /ɪ/ is used to transcribe "ing" as in "making" [mekɪŋ] or "thing" [θɪŋ].

You may have the temptation to use the [i] before /ŋ/, but resist! Compare the difference between the sound of /i/ in "meat" [mit], or "three" [θri] to the /i/ in [iŋ], and you will hear that the vowel does not sound the same.

Another important consideration is the *phonetic environment* of the high front vowel when it is adjacent to a nasal sound. Phonetic environment is defined as the phonemes that surround a specific speech sound. The /ŋ/ is a nasal consonant that requires nasal resonance through opening of the velopharyngeal port. Since the "i" gains nasal resonance, it can also cause it to sound more like /ɪ/ rather than /i/.

Remember that this rule only applies to "i-ng" orthographically and not to any other vowels before "ng" as in "sang" [sæŋ] or "strong" [strɑŋ].

NASALS

Word Search #4   Answers in Appendix B

ʃ	d	l	ɔ	p	n	b	ʌ	dʒ	ʃ	ɪ	r	ʒ
æ	ŋ	k	ɚ	r	k	z	æ	ɝ	j	ɝ	ɛ	o
d	s	dʒ	ʒ	t	θ	tʃ	ɪ	d	ɔ	b	k	ə
ɪ	ɑ	n	ɝ	ɔ	ʌ	r	m	r	h	ɛ	t	k
k	j	æ	ŋ	k	ɪ	ŋ	b	ɪ	ə	s	æ	b
d	t	k	d	l	ŋ	t	s	ŋ	o	l	ŋ	ɪ
ɪ	m	m	ʃ	ə	s	i	ɪ	k	ə	b	g	e
s	l	ɪ	ŋ	g	ɚ	m	tʃ	ə	i	z	ə	w
ŋ	k	ə	w	n	z	w	ʃ	e	tʃ	d	l	i
ʃ	l	ɪ	n	i	k	m	ʌ	ŋ	k	n	ð	æ
l	ɛ	h	ð	l	o	d	r	l	ɛ	s	t	t
ʃ	ŋ	l	o	ɪ	l	æ	e	e	o	d	ɛ	l
æ	k	m	tʃ	ŋ	g	b	s	w	ɪ	ŋ	z	i
p	θ	r	z	k	n	θ	ɪ	i	u	tʃ	d	z
h	ɪ	s	s	ʒ	s	r	ŋ	m	n	r	k	ɪ

Directions: Find and circle the words listed below that contain the /ŋ/.

linger	monk
length	racing
swings	rectangle
link	anchor
drink	yanking

Crossword Puzzle for /m/, /n/, and /ŋ/

Answers in Appendix B

1					2	
3						
4						

Directions: Transcribe the following words:

Across:

1. nine
3. kingdom
4. pneumonia

Down:

1. napkin
2. steam

Syllabics

In its simplest form, a syllabic is a consonant with a vowel-like quality. A syllabic consonant acts like a vowel. For example, the word "hidden" can be pronounced in two ways: (a) [hɪdən] or (b) [hɪdn̩]. In the first example, the tongue *leaves* the alveolar ridge after producing /d/ to produce the midcentral schwa vowel, and then returns to the alveolar ridge to produce /n/. In the second example, the tongue *remains* on the alveolar ridge after production of /d/ to produce the following syllabic /n̩/.

To change a consonant to a syllabic, a diacritic is used. A small vertical line (‚) is placed under the consonant. Remember that the diacritic (‚) *replaces* a vowel. No vowel will precede a syllabic consonant or appear in the same syllable where a syllabic occurs.

The use of syllabics is variable, depending on the speaker. Syllabics occur more frequently in conversational speech, as they facilitate rapid rate of speech.

Syllabics serve as the center (nucleus) of a syllable. The /m̩/n̩/ŋ̩/l̩/ can function as a syllabic. Consonant syllabics function in unstressed syllables in words of two or more syllables. All vowels are syllabics.

The use of syllabics occurs in conversational speech and in producing the words in isolation, as in the example with "hidden." The /m̩/, /n̩/, and /ŋ̩/ syllabics share a homorganic (made in the same place of articulation) relationship with the previous phoneme. For example, the syllabic /m̩/ will follow /b/ and /p/ because they are made in the bilabial place of production. The syllabic /n̩/ can follow the lingua-alveolar productions of /t/d/s/z/. The syllabic /ŋ̩/ can follow the lingua-velar /k/ and /g/. The syllabic /l̩/ can follow any consonant (Edwards, 2003). Examples of these syllabics:

	Word	Transcription
Syllabic /m/	open	[opm̩]
Syllabic /n/	reason	[rizn̩]
Syllabic /ŋ/	broken	[brokŋ̩]
Syllabic /l/	medal	[mɛdl̩]

Transcription Exercise 5–8 provides an opportunity to listen to syllabic consonants used in formal and casual speech.

Transcription Exercise 5–7

Nasal Consonants / m / n / ŋ /

🔊 **AUDIO 1–26**

Phoneme Study Cards: 19–21

1. nasal   _____

2. monumental   _____

3. among   _____

4. remnant   _____

5. nominate   _____

6. feminine   _____

7. lemonade   _____

8. morning   _____

9. chimney   _____

10. meeting   _____

11. containing _____

12. mingling   _____

13. membrane   _____

14. money   _____

15. nanny   _____

16. meringue   _____

17. mountain   _____

18. numerical   _____

19. cinnamon   _____

20. moonbeam   _____

Transcription Exercise 5–8  **AUDIO 1–27**

This exercise will give you practice in identifying syllabics as used in formal and casual speech. The word will first be pronounced as it would in formal speech, and then in casual speech. Listen carefully as some of these differences can be subtle. You may think that you've never said a word in that way, especially using syllabic /ŋ̩/ and /m̩/, but this is good practice. Words are transcribed for you in Appendix B.

	Formal Speech	Casual Speech
1. cabin		
2. medal		
3. redden		
4. ribbon		
5. blacken		
6. panel		
7. milking		
8. garden		
9. broken		
10. open		

STUDY QUESTIONS

1. What are the nasal consonants?

_____

_____

2. How does place of production for each of the nasal consonants differ?

_____

_____

3. Define homorganic.

_____

_____

4. What is a syllabic consonant?

_____

_____

5. Define the difference between formal and casual speech.

_____

_____

6. List the homorganic phoneme relationships for /n/m/ and /ŋ/.

_____

_____

7. What diacritic is used to indicate a syllabic? Give an example using a syllabic consonant.

_____

_____

CHAPTER

6

Consonants: Fricatives /s/z/f/v/ʃ/ʒ/θ/ð/h/hw/

Learning Objectives

After reading this chapter, you will be able to:

1. Explain the difference between production of stop-consonants and fricatives.

2. State tongue and lip positions for interdentals and labiodentals.

3. List spelling variations for /f/.

4. Describe two tongue positions for /s/ and /z/.

5. Transcribe words using fricative consonants.

As discussed in Chapter 3, fricatives are produced when the breath stream passes through a narrow constriction in the vocal tract. Unlike the stop-consonants that are produced with a complete obstruction of the breath stream, fricatives are produced with a *partial* blockage of the airstream.

Each fricative has a voiced cognate, with the exception of /h/ and /hw/. These phonemes are classified as fricatives, but are not considered cognates as both phonemes are unvoiced when produced in isolation. Unlike the oral cavity, which is the source of friction for the majority of the fricatives, the glottis serves as the source of friction for the /h/ and /hw/.

/f/

Transcription Exercise 6–1   🔊)) **AUDIO 1–28**

		I	M	F
1.	phosphorus			
2.	pamphlet			
3.	giraffe			
4.	photo			
5.	fifteen			
6.	Joseph			
7.	spherical			
8.	monograph			
9.	fluffy			
10.	phonograph			

Transcription Exercise 6–2

Consonant: /f/

🔊 **AUDIO 1–29**

Refer to Study Card: 9

Phonetic Symbol	Target Word	Transcription
/f/	1. fun	
	2. before	
	3. fifteen	
	4. frost	
	5. coffee	
	6. leaf	
	7. laugh	
	8. float	
	9. if	

/f/

Distinctive Features	Tongue Position
Labio-dental fricative Unvoiced, front, labial, nonsonorant, continuant, nonsibilant, nonnasal 	Inner border of lower lip is raised to contact upper incisors. Breath stream is continuously emitted between upper teeth and lower lip, creating friction. Tongue position is irrelevant; may be in position for following phoneme.

Voicing/Velopharyngeal Port	Spelling Variations
Voiceless—vocal folds *ab*duct. VP port is closed.	ff is transcribed as single /f/ as in co*ff*ee. ph *phone*, pro*ph*et gh rou*gh*, lau*gh*

Word Positions	Clinical Information
Initial, medial, and final positions in SAE	Common articulatory substitutions: p/f, b/f Cognate of /v/

/v/

Transcription Exercise 6–3

 **AUDIO 1–30**

		I	M	F
1.	vindictive			
2.	wife			
3.	chevron			
4.	weaver			
5.	of			
6.	lifesaving			
7.	never			
8.	wives			
9.	verify			
10.	stove			

Transcription Exercise 6–4

🔊)) AUDIO 1–31

Consonant: /v/

Refer to Study Card: 10

Phonetic Symbol	Target Word	Transcription
/v/	1. vine	
	2. velvet	
	3. over	
	4. very	
	5. invite	
	6. live	
	7. value	
	8. weaver	
	9. move	

/v/

Distinctive Features	Tongue Position
Labio-dental fricative	See /f/ for description of production.
Voiced front, labial, nonsonorant, continuant, nonsibilant, nonnasal	

/v/ ——→

Voicing/Velopharyngeal Port	Spelling Variations
Voiced—vocal folds *ad*duct.	ph Ste*ph*en
VP port is closed.	lv silent /l/ as in ca*l*ves, sa*l*ves

Word Positions	Clinical Information
Initial, medial, and final positions in SAE	Substituted with /b/ or omitted
	Cognate of /f/

Crossword Puzzle for /f/ and /v/

See Answers in Appendix B

Directions: Transcribe the following words:

Across:

1. caffeine
4. vase
5. flip

Down:

1. cavity
2. festival
3. notify

MONDAY NIGHT FOOTBALL

Word Search #5   Answers in Appendix B

v	ɪ	k	t	ɔ	r	i	h	e	d	ɪ	n
m	h	ɛ	g	d	e	t	r	r	b	s	h
ɑ	r	r	ɪ	t	ɚ	m	ɛ	i	n	k	ɛ
r	ɛ	ə	v	ɪ	n	s	k	s	ɑ	k	p
s	f	ʊ	t	b	ɔ	l	i	i	l	ɪ	d
u	ɚ	n	d	h	ɑ	r	v	v	i	k	ə
n	i	ə	s	e	f	t	i	ɚ	t	ɔ	h
b	l	u	d	w	ɪ	i	v	g	u	f	æ
f	ʊ	l	b	æ	k	l	ɑ	m	p	r	f
r	w	f	ɑ	d	s	w	r	θ	ɛ	e	b
ʊ	u	i	dʒ	d	ə	ʃ	s	ɛ	r	n	æ
k	d	l	u	æ	m	æ	ɪ	r	i	i	k
s	b	d	l	i	t	m	t	i	dʒ	ɛ	r
ɔ	f	ɛ	n	s	ɑ	d	i	f	ɛ	n	s

Directions: Find and circle the words listed below that contain the /f/ or /v/ phonemes.

referee	kickoff	fullback
football	varsity	field
victory	receiver	defense
safety	halfback	offense

/s/

Transcription Exercise 6–5   🔊 **AUDIO 1–32**

		I	M	F
1.	city			
2.	shaves			
3.	deceptive			
4.	blintz			
5.	usual			
6.	axes			
7.	bracelet			
8.	island			
9.	pseudo			
10.	Bronx			

Transcription Exercise 6–6   🔊 **AUDIO 1–33**

Consonant: /s/   Refer to Study Card: 7

Phonetic Symbol	Target Word	Transcription
/s/	1. else	
	2. asleep	
	3. superior	
	4. basin	
	5. Easter	
	6. cedar	
	7. asks	
	8. sandal	
	9. blast	

/s/

Distinctive Features	Tongue Position
Lingua-alveolar fricative Voiceless, front, nonlabial, nonsonorant, continuant, sibilant, nonnasal 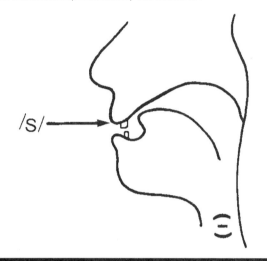	Tongue tip up: Tongue tip, narrowly grooved, contacts alveolar ridge behind *upper* incisors. Breath is continuously directed through narrow aperture between alveolar ridge and grooved tongue tip, creating turbulence. Tongue tip down: Tip of tongue contacts alveolar ridge behind *lower* incisors. Front of tongue, slightly grooved, is raised toward alveolar ridge, and forms a narrow aperture through which breath is continuously directed against front teeth, creating turbulence. Lips are apart and neutral; may be in position for following vowel.

Voicing/Velopharyngeal Port	Spelling Variations
Voiceless—vocal folds *ab*duct. VP port is closed.	Variable spelling Pronounced as /z/ in busine*s*s, /ʒ/ in trea*s*ure, /ʃ/ as in *s*ure x /ks/ as in wa*x*, fi*x* c as /s/ sound in *c*ity, *c*ycle sc *sc*epter, *sc*ene st with silent /t/ as in gli*st*en, tre*st*le ps silent /p/ as in *p*sychology s as plural form, present tense, or possessive, after voiceless consonant as in cape*s*, sit*s*, Pat'*s*

Word Position	Clinical Information
Initial, medial, and final positions in SAE	This phoneme is frequently misarticulated. One of the most frequently occurring consonants in SAE Common substitutions include /t/ /d/ or /ʃ/. Interdental lisp: substituted with /θ/ (tip of tongue protrudes between teeth) Lateral lisp: airflow *around* tongue rather than through front of oral cavity Cognate of /z/

/z/

Transcription Exercise 6–7   🔊 **AUDIO 1–34**

		I	M	F
1.	kids			
2.	czar			
3.	cheese			
4.	observe			
5.	business			
6.	nasal			
7.	present			
8.	is			
9.	seizure			
10.	bobsleds			

Transcription Exercise 6–8

🔊 **AUDIO 1–35**

Consonant: /z/

Refer to Study Card: 8

Phonetic Symbol	Target Word	Transcription
/z/	1. busy	
	2. visit	
	3. zircon	
	4. weasel	
	5. seas	
	6. zinnia	
	7. those	
	8. zucchini	
	9. gives	

/z/

Distinctive Features	Tongue Position
Lingua–alveolar fricative Voiced, front, nonlabial, nonsonorant, continuant, sibilant, nonnasal / Z / →	See /s/ for description of production.

Voicing/Velopharyngeal Port	Spelling Variations
Voiced—vocal folds *ad*duct. VP port is closed.	s as in hi*s*, wa*s*, de*s*ign, scissor*s* es plural forms or possessive as in kiss*es*, boy'*s* ss occurs as /z/ in sci*ss*ors. sth a*sth*ma x *x*ylophone x forms /gz/ in e*x*amine [ɛgzæmɪn].

Word Position	Clinical Information
Initial, medial, and final positions in SAE	Commonly substituted with /d/ or /t/. Can also be produced as interdental or lateral lisp (see /s/ Clinical Information). Cognate of /s/

CAN YOU HEAR THE DIFFERENCE BETWEEN /s/ AND /z/?

Listening Exercise Final /z/    AUDIO 1–36

It is not always easy to *hear* the difference between /s/ and /z/, especially in the final position of words. As you listen to the audio file, pay attention to the /z/. The /z/ is emphasized in these words:

1. phase	16. news
2. cheese	17. sees
3. surprise	18. pies
4. fleas	19. rituals
5. tease	20. bruise
6. was	21. Eloise
7. tragedies	22. joys
8. wise	23. cardinals
9. rose	24. Japanese
10. bananas	25. is
11. cruise	26. tomatoes
12. eyes	27. skis
13. glows	28. kneels
14. choose	29. stereos
15. goes	30. advertise

Crossword Puzzle for /s/ and /z/

Answers in Appendix B

Directions: Transcribe the following words:

Across:

3. zip
4. sizzle
5. soldier

Down:

1. soups
2. zeal
3. Zorro
3. seasons

THE CENTER RING

Word Search #6

Answers in Appendix B

æ	h	m	s	t	o	ɑ	g	ɪ	t	m	k
k	æ	ɛ	l	ə	f	ɪ	n	t	s	z	ɑ
r	m	t	i	ɚ	r	h	d	r	k	ɛ	s
o	h	p	s	ɛ	ks	aɪ	t	m	ɛ	n	t
b	u	ɛ	ə	m	i	d	r	ɛ	o	tʃ	u
æ	t	r	m	ɛ	ə	h	æ	k	r	ə	m
t	b	i	s	m	l	aʊ	p	i	n	i	z
s	ɝ	k	ə	s	d	r	i	t	p	ɑ	l
j	ɑ	h	ɪ	k	e	g	z	i	b	r	ə
h	ð	æ	r	l	l	e	e	u	o	k	ɑ
u	k	l	k	aʊ	e	t	aɪ	g	ɚ	z	r
p	æ	o	n	n	b	d	dʒ	d	t	o	z
s	t	w	l	z	n	ɔ	ɝ	i	e	t	i
s	l	aɪ	ə	n	z	r	t	ɛ	n	t	s

Directions: Find and circle the words listed below that contain the /s/ or /z/ phonemes.

circus	clowns	acrobats
trapeze	zebra	lions
costumes	excitement	elephants
tigers	hoops	tents

Transcription Exercise 6–9

Fricative Consonants: / f / v / s / z /

1. festive   _____

2. Swiss   _____

3. vessel   _____

4. fanciful   _____

5. measles   _____

6. zest   _____

7. vivid   _____

8. expensive   _____

9. businesses   _____

10. forgive   _____

11. soapsuds   _____

12. fasten   _____

13. squeeze   _____

14. scissors   _____

15. pharmacy   _____

16. Stephen   _____

17. vice   _____

18. Switzerland   _____

19. safety   _____

20. civilian   _____

/θ/

Transcription Exercise 6–10   🔊 AUDIO 1–38

		I	M	F
1.	enthusiast			
2.	Thursday			
3.	thither			
4.	Elizabeth			
5.	thirty-third			
6.	Gothic			
7.	cathedral			
8.	through			
9.	anesthesia			
10.	zenith			

Transcription Exercise 6–11

Consonant: /θ/

Refer to Study Card: 11

Phonetic Symbol	Target Word	Transcription
/θ/	1. thin	θɪn
	2. birthday	bɝθdeɪ
	3. width	wɪdθ
	4. teeth	tiθ
	5. throw	θroʊ
	6. anything	ɛniθɪŋ
	7. north	nɔrθ
	8. nothing	nʌθɪŋ
	9. thaw	θɔ

For #3 wɪdθ or wɪθ is acceptable

/θ/

Distinctive Features	Tongue Position
Interdental fricative Voiceless, front, nonlabial, nonsonorant, continuant, nonsibilant, nonnasal /θ/ ⟶	Sides of tongue are against upper molars. Tip and blade of tongue are spread wide and thin in space between teeth. Breath is continuously emitted between front teeth. Lips are apart and neutral.

Voicing/Velopharyngeal Port	Spelling Variations
Voiceless—vocal folds *ab*duct. VP port is closed.	th is the only spelling th ba*th*, mon*th* th some*th*ing, au*th*or thr *th*ree

Word Positions	Clinical Information
Initial, medial, and final positions in SAE	Also known as "theta" A sound unique to the English language (Edwards, 2003) Commonly substituted with /t/s/f/ Cognate of /ð/

/ð/

Transcription Exercise 6–12   🔊 **AUDIO 1–40**

		I	M	F
1.	them			
2.	clothe			
3.	Heather			
4.	rhythm			
5.	teeth			
6.	north			
7.	whether			
8.	thigh			
9.	northern			
10.	weather			

Transcription Exercise 6–13

Consonant: /ð/

🔊)) **AUDIO 1–41**

Refer to Study Card: 12

Phonetic Symbol		Target Word	Transcription
/ð/		1. this	ðɪs
	X	2. either	iðər
		3. there	ðɛr
	X	4. father	faðər
		5. seethe	si ð
		6. though	ðoʊ
	X	7. mother	mʌðər
		8. teethe	tið
		9. smooth	smuð

corrections
2. iðɚ
4. faðɚ
7. mʌðɚ

✻Transcription
website doesn't
transcribe
"er/ur" properly

/ð/

Distinctive Features	Tongue Position
Interdental fricative Voiced front, nonlabial, nonsonorant, continuant, nonsibilant, nonnasal /ð/ ⟶	Same tongue position as for production of /θ/

Voicing/Velopharyngeal Port	Spelling Variations
Voiced—vocal folds *ad*ducted. VP port is closed.	th is the only spelling th occurs in frequently used words such as *the, this, that, they, them, then, these, there, those.* th ba*the*, soo*the*, bo*ther*, fea*ther*

Word Positions	Clinical Information
Initial, medial, and final positions in SAE	A sound unique to the English language (Edwards, 2003) Commonly substituted with /d/ and /t/ Cognate of /θ/

Transcription Exercise 6–14    **AUDIO 1–42**

It is often difficult for beginning phonetics students to hear the difference between the voiced "th" /ð/ and unvoiced "th" /θ/. It can be helpful if you say words with these phonemes to "feel" the difference. When you pronounce the voiced "th," you will feel a vibration produced by the tongue placement between the central incisors. In addition, the vocal folds vibrate. Contrast this production with the unvoiced "th" in which there is no vocal fold vibration. Directions: Say each word and write the symbol for the voiced /ð/ or unvoiced /θ/ phoneme. Listen to the audio files if you need help.

1. wreathe (verb)
2. than
3. earthworm
4. bath
5. ungathered
6. seethe
7. stethoscope
8. blithe
9. amethyst
10. featherbed
11. weatherman
12. locksmith
13. with
14. though
15. either

16. thank
17. although
18. thou
19. rhythm
20. pathway
21. Judith
22. healthy
23. marathon
24. together
25. thump
26. Southerner
27. these
28. either
29. lather
30. Keith

Crossword Puzzle for /θ/ and /ð/

Answers in Appendix B

Directions: Transcribe the following words:

Across:
1. father
2. those
3. mothers
4. thin
6. rhythm

Down:
1. feathers
3. methodic
5. north

INTERDENTAL FRICATIVE

Word Search #7   Answers in Appendix B

g   t   k   ɛ   l   v   b   ʌ   k   b   m   s

ɝ   ʒ   p   æ   θ   h   e   b   m   ɛ   θ   aʊ

k   p   o   r   ɛ   e   ð   ɛ   ɪ   d   ð   d

l   p   θ   t   m   v   m   ɛ   o   e   æ   m

o   o   r   æ   ð   b   ɑ   ð   ɚ   l   n   ɑ

ð   k   ɛ   n   p   f   θ   l   d   t   t   m

e   θ   d   d   ə   n   ə   ð   ɚ   p   æ   æ

v   n   k   m   g   tʃ   æ   t   ə   k   n   θ

æ   ɚ   ð   g   r   θ   ɪ   ŋ   l   l   r   ɪ

θ   n   t   æ   ɝ   ɝ   θ   ɚ   z   ɑ   t   ɛ

r   g   n   ð   v   d   r   w   ɪ   θ   aʊ   t

j   b   o   ɚ   k   h   ɪ   b   s   e   t   i

ə   æ   g   m   s   aʊ   θ   ɑ   l   m   ɛ   g

t   θ   t   θ   p   z   n   r   i   æ   n   k

Directions: Find and circle the words listed below that contain the /θ/ or /ð/ phonemes.

thread	moth	than	cloth
third	without	bother	clothe
thing	math	bath	path
south	another	bathe	gather

Transcription Exercise 6–15

Interdental Consonants: / θ / ð /

🔊 **AUDIO 1–43**

Phoneme Study Cards: 11–12

 1. bike-a-thon   _____

 2. Wadsworth   _____

 3. southeastern   _____

 4. arithmetic   _____

 5. seventeenth   _____

 6. threaten   _____

 7. undergrowth   _____

 8. southernmost   _____

 9. Thunderbird   _____

10. Plymouth   _____

11. ruthlessly   _____

12. Witherspoon   _____

13. heartthrob   _____

14. worthy   _____

15. thriving   _____

16. another   _____

17. methodic   _____

18. thoughtless   _____

19. hundredth   _____

20. leather   _____

/h/

Transcription Exercise 6–16   🔊)) **AUDIO 1–44**

		I	M	F
1.	whom			
2.	rehearse			
3.	hitchhike			
4.	unwholesome			
5.	Jose			
6.	inhale			
7.	Gila monster			
8.	habitat			
9.	mahogany			
10.	exhalation			

Transcription Exercise 6–17

🔊)) AUDIO 1–45

Consonant: /h/

Refer to Study Card: 15

Phonetic Symbol	Target Word	Transcription
/h/	1. heft	
	2. harbor	
	3. mohair	
	4. uphill	
	5. hum	
	6. inherit	
	7. rehearse	
	8. hermit	
	9. unhook	

/h/

Distinctive Features	Tongue Position
Glottal fricative Voiceless, back, nonlabial, nonsonorant, continuant, nonsibilant, nonnasal /h/ ←	No consistent articulatory pattern. Tongue and lips are in position for following phoneme. Turbulence is created at level of glottis. Breath is directed through the oral cavity.

Voicing/Velopharyngeal Port	Spelling Variations
If produced in isolation, /h/ is voiceless—vocal folds are *ab*ducted. VP port is closed.	wh *wh*om, *wh*ole gh silent as in Hu*gh* h silent in *h*onor, *h*onest

Word Positions	Clinical Information
Initial and medial positions in SAE	May be replaced with glottal stop in certain dialects.

/hw/ or /ʍ/

Transcription Exercise 6–18

 **AUDIO 1–46**

		I	M	F
1.	wheel			
2.	queen			
3.	swear			
4.	why			
5.	suede			
6.	where			
7.	whole wheat			
8.	wear			
9.	wagon			
10.	square			

Note. Although use of this phoneme is not common, it is helpful for purposes of "ear training" to discriminate between /hw/ and /w/. With the exception of "wear" and "wagon," the remainder of the words in this exercise can be produced with /hw/ as an alternative pronunciation.

Transcription Exercise 6–19   🔊 **AUDIO 1–47**

Consonant: /hw/ also /ʍ/   Refer to Study Card: 16

Phonetic Symbol	Target Word	Transcription
/hw/	1. whim	
	2. overwhelm	
	3. whip	
	4. twenty	
	5. schwa	
	6. white	
	7. somewhere	
	8. whether	
	9. wharf	

/hw/ or /ʍ/

Distinctive Features	Tongue Position
Labial-velar (bilabial) fricative Voiceless, nonsibilant, continuant 	Back of tongue may be raised toward soft palate, or may be in low back position for /h/. Lips may be rounded. Breath is directed through oral cavity and lip opening.
Voicing/Velopharyngeal Port	**Spelling Variations**
Voiceless; however, vocal folds *ad*duct slightly to create turbulence. VP port is closed.	w following /s/ as in s*w*im, s*w*ag; following /t/ as in t*w*ig, t*w*elve, and following "th" as in th*w*art, may be produced with the /ʍ/ wh *wh*eel, some*wh*ere
Word Positions	**Clinical Information**
Initial and medial positions in SAE	Also called inverted "w" Most commonly produced as /w/

Transcription Exercise 6–20

Consonants: /h/hw/ or /ʍ/

1. hedgehog   _____

2. suede   _____

3. whirl   _____

4. whom   _____

5. sway   _____

6. wahoo   _____

7. whine   _____

8. handshake   _____

9. hair   _____

10. whiff   _____

11. who   _____

12. whammy   _____

13. wholehearted   _____

14. where   _____

15. pinwheel   _____

16. hymn   _____

17. persuade   _____

18. whistle   _____

19. Ohio   _____

20. whose   _____

/ʃ/

Transcription Exercise 6–21

 **AUDIO 1–49**

		I	M	F
1.	condition			
2.	usher			
3.	tissue			
4.	brochure			
5.	chiffon			
6.	initial			
7.	treasure			
8.	licorice			
9.	creation			
10.	shoe brush			

Transcription Exercise 6–22

Consonant: /ʃ/

🔊 AUDIO 1–50

Refer to Study Card: 13

Phonetic Symbol	Target Word	Transcription
/ʃ/	1. shoe	
	2. mustache	
	3. ocean	
	4. insure	
	5. wish	
	6. ship	
	7. relish	
	8. shake	
	9. fashion	

/ʃ/

Distinctive Features	Articulatory Production
Lingua-palatal fricative	Sides of tongue contact upper molars.
Voiceless, back, nonsonorant, continuant, sibilant, nonnasal	Tip of tongue is at the lower central incisors; front of tongue raised toward hard palate.
	Breath stream is directed through and against slightly opened front teeth to create audible friction.
	Lips are slightly rounded and protruded, approximating position for /ʊ/.

Voicing/Velopharyngeal Port	Spelling Variations
Voiceless—vocal folds *ab*duct.	s *s*ugar, in*s*urance
VP port is closed.	c o*c*ean
	ch *ch*ic, musta*ch*e
	tion na*tion*, ac*tion*
	sc con*sc*ience
	chs fu*chs*ia

Word Positions	Clinical Information
Initial, medial, and final positions in SAE	Common articulatory substitution: t/ʃ, d/ʃ, s/ʃ
	Cognate of /ʒ/

/ʒ/

Transcription Exercise 6–23　　　　　　🔊 **AUDIO 1–51**

		I	M	F
1.	vision			
2.	aphasia			
3.	garage			
4.	station			
5.	treasure			
6.	Persia			
7.	closure			
8.	rouge			
9.	composure			
10.	television			

Note. #3, garage, may also be produced as [gʌradʒ].

Transcription Exercise 6–24

Consonant: /ʒ/

🔊 **AUDIO 1–52**

Refer to Study Card: 14

Phonetic Symbol	Target Word	Transcription
/ʒ/	1. regime	
	2. loge	
	3. pleasure	
	4. division	
	5. usual	
	6. collision	
	7. beige	
	8. collage	
	9. casual	

/ʒ/

Distinctive Features	Tongue Position
Lingua-palatal fricative Voiced, back, nonlabial, nonsonorant, continuant, sibilant, nonnasal	See /ʃ/ for description of production.

Voicing/Velopharyngeal Port	Spelling Variations
Voiced—vocal folds *ad*duct. VP port is closed.	s as in measure, occasion g(e) bei*ge*, presti*ge* z azure, seizure

Word Positions	Clinical Information
Medial and final positions in SAE	Common articulation error is substitution of /d/, /t/, and omission Cognate of /ʃ/

Crossword Puzzle for /ʃ/ and /ʒ/

Answers in Appendix B

1		2				

Directions: Transcribe the following words:

Across:
1. vacation
3. leisure
4. aphasia
6. shun

Down:
2. collision
5. fish

UNDER THE SEA

Word Search #8   Answers in Appendix B

ʃ	æ	l	o	k	ʃ	s	z	n	æ	aɪ	p
d	d	d	p	r	r	ɪ	ɪ	k	n	g	ɔ
ɪ	l	ʌ	æ	o	ɪ	t	k	θ	o	l	l
k	n	k	n	j	m	i	l	ɪ	ʃ	k	ə
d	r	m	ʃ	ɪ	p	s	s	ŋ	ə	r	n
ɪ	ɑ	ə	d	u	r	m	l	s	n	ɑ	i
s	d	ɪ	s	n	o	ə	z	z	d	f	ʒ
n	s	n	d	t	f	ɪ	ʃ	k	r	ɚ	ə
ʃ	o	l	e	θ	e	ð	ɔ	o	u	j	k
i	m	m	l	w	z	ʃ	ə	l	ʃ	æ	d
ʃ	ɑ	r	k	d	i	l	ə	h	w	b	o
l	i	s	p	r	o	n	ð	n	ɛ	r	l
æ	t	r	ɛ	ʒ	ɚ	tʃ	ɛ	s	t	t	æ
p	m	k	l	æ	m	ʃ	ɛ	l	b	m	b
h	ɪ	tʃ	u	o	d	ɔ	ə	s	ɚ	ɪ	ʒ
d	k	ɪ	z	b	ʌ	r	l	ɛ	m	n	r

Directions: Find and circle the words listed below that contain the /ʃ/ or /ʒ/ phonemes.

shrimp	treasure chest	shallow	ships
shore	crustacean	shark	fish
clamshell	ocean	shoal	shad
Polynesia			

STUDY QUESTIONS

1. Why are the /h/ and /hw/ classified as fricatives but are not cognates?

   _____

   _____

2. What is the source of friction for the /h/ and /hw/?

   _____

   _____

3. What is the tongue position for production of /f/ and /v/?

   _____

   _____

4. What are two ways the /s/ and /z/ can be produced?

   _____

   _____

5. What is the difference between an interdental lisp and a lateral lisp?

   _____

   _____

6. What is the Greek name for the voiceless "th"?

   _____

   _____

7. What is the tongue position for production of /ʃ/ and /ʒ/?

   _____

   _____

CHAPTER

7

Consonants: Affricates /tʃ/dʒ/

Learning Objectives

After reading this chapter, you will be able to:

1. Describe how affricates are produced.

2. Identify manner of production of affricates.

3. Explain how to correctly write the two components of the affricates.

4. List spelling variations for the affricates.

5. Transcribe words using affricate consonants.

The affricates are a combination of a stop-consonant immediately followed by a fricative, produced in the same breath. They are also called "stop-fricatives," which describes their manner of production. Affricates are considered obstruents as they are produced with an obstructed breath stream.

Some phoneticians prefer to write the two components of the affricates touching each other to emphasize that they are produced with a single breath impulse and to eliminate confusing the symbols with two separate phonemes.

/ʧ/

Transcription Exercise 7–1

◀)) **AUDIO 1–53**

		I	M	F
1.	chef			
2.	hatchet			
3.	pitch			
4.	brochure			
5.	chord			
6.	culture			
7.	ache			
8.	machine			
9.	church			
10.	future			

Transcription Exercise 7–2

🔊 **AUDIO 1–54**

Consonant: /tʃ/

Refer to Study Card: 17

Phonetic Symbol	Target Word	Transcription
/tʃ/	1. chin	
	2. peaches	
	3. which	
	4. cheese	
	5. lunch	
	6. teacher	
	7. children	
	8. scotch	
	9. furniture	

/ʧ/

Distinctive Features	Tongue Position
Alveopalatal affricate	Sides of tongue against upper molars
Voiceless, back, nonlabial, nonsonorant, noncontinuant, sibilant, nonnasal	Tip and blade of tongue close on or just behind upper alveolar ridge
	Air held and compressed in oral cavity; exploded as audible breath through broad opening between alveolar ridge and front of tongue.
	Turbulence is created.
	Lips are apart and neutral.
	The phoneme begins as a stop /t/ with tongue moving into position for /ʃ/.

Voicing/Velopharyngeal Port	Spelling Variations
Voiceless—vocal folds *ab*duct.	tch *match, catch*
VP port is closed.	t(ure) frac*ture*, furni*ture*
	t(ion) men*tion*, ques*tion*
	nsion with intruded /t/ for /nʧ/ as in te*nsion* [tɛntʃən]
	t(u) vir*tue*, na*tural*
	Infrequently with c as in *cello*

Word Position	Clinical Information
Initial, medial, and final positions in SAE	Common articulation error of substitution of /t/ or /d/ or omitted
	Cognate of /dʒ/

/dʒ/

Transcription Exercise 7–3    **AUDIO 1–55**

		I	M	F
1.	garage			
2.	budget			
3.	ginger			
4.	dungeon			
5.	jump			
6.	education			
7.	gesture			
8.	voyage			
9.	engine			
10.	splurge			

Transcription Exercise 7–4

Consonant: /dʒ/

🔊 **AUDIO 1–56**

Refer to Study Card: 18

Phonetic Symbol	Target Word	Transcription
/dʒ/	1. junk	
	2. enjoy	
	3. urged	
	4. vigil	
	5. wage	
	6. gem	
	7. jumbo	
	8. collagen	
	9. fudge	

/dʒ/

Distinctive Features	Tongue Position
Alveopalatal affricate Voiced, back, nonlabial, nonsonorant, noncontinuant, sibilant, nonnasal 	See /tʃ/ for production. This phoneme begins as a stop /d/ with tongue moving into position for /ʒ/.

Voicing/Velopharyngeal Port	Spelling Variations
Voiced—vocal folds *ad*duct. VP port is closed.	gg exa*gg*erate d cor*d*ial, gra*d*ual j *j*uice, *j*erk dge e*dge* g tra*g*ic, en*g*ine, *g*ypsy dj a*dj*ust

Word Position	Clinical Information
Initial, medial, and final positions in SAE	Cognate of /tʃ/

Crossword Puzzle for /tʃ/ and /dʒ/

Answers in Appendix B

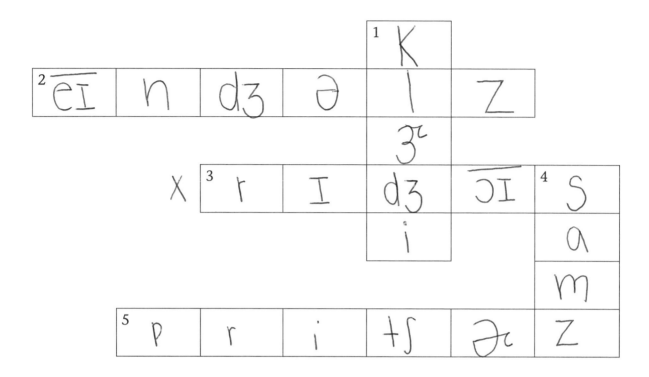

Directions: Transcribe the following words:

Across:

2. angels
3. rejoice
5. preachers

Down:

1. clergy
4. psalms

2. eɪndʒəlz

X 3. rɪdʒɔɪs

5. pritʃɚz

1. klɝdʒi

4. samz

corrections

3. rədʒɔɪs ʊr rɪdʒɔɪs

AFFRICATES

Word Search #9   Answers in Appendix B

```
k   p   ɑ   s   s   ɑ   g   e   z   e   dʒ  i   p   b   r   j   m   ɛ
n   k   w   tʃ  k   v   u   i   tʃ  kʍ  o   f   z   g   j   r   s   n
d   b   t   s   i   ə   b   ɛ   ks  tʃ  e   n   dʒ  n   u   tʃ  v   d
j   s   p   k   æ   z   h   v   s   t   o   h   i   g   m   v   ɪ   z
m   j   æ   h   u   h   ɑ   h   w   n   ɛ   w   f   dʒ  p   r   l   t
p   æ   d   v   ɛ   n   tʃ  ɚ   k   θ   u   p   ʌ   z   s   p   ɪ   m
m   e   ɔ   z   v   l   ɝ   p   æ   s   ɪ   dʒ  ɛ   p   o   k   dʒ  n
m   m   ʒ   h   p   b   f   o   g   s   t   ʃ   dʒ  h   w   g   g   ŋ
g   ɑ   dʒ  ɪ   ŋ   k   s   s   t   z   æ   l   ɪ   o   e   æ   ʌ   ɑ
t   v   ɪ   f   k   g   θ   ɔ   d   ʃ   l   k   ʊ   j   h   s   ʊ   ʍ
v   d   l   i   æ   o   n   d   dʒ  h   l   m   f   v   ʌ   s   ə   j
t   f   ɛ   r   ʌ   i   ʒ   r   n   ʒ   f   æ   æ   z   f   n   s   r
r   b   r   ɪ   dʒ  ɛ   z   l   ɪ   m   z   dʒ  p   ɛ   ɪ   b   z   l
j   b   w   e   ɪ   f   ŋ   ɪ   l   n   m   ɪ   v   ks  h   i   ʃ   ʌ
i   w   o   o   k   v   ɛ   ʊ   æ   ŋ   d   k   m   u   w   tʃ  h   ɛ
l   n   h   r   ʃ   ð   n   ɚ   tʃ  ɔ   o   v   h   n   j   p   ʒ   p
ʊ   z   s   ɪ   n   tʃ  ə   p   f   o   s   p   ɛ   h   t   i   tʃ  t
z   h   t   u   t   h   ʍ   b   v   u   n   ʒ   l   m   r   w   dʒ  d
```

Directions: Find and circle the words below that contain the /tʃ/ and /dʒ/ phonemes.

cheese	jinx	age	cinch
challenge	judge	adventure	village
exchange	magic	passage	
beach	bridges	teach	

Transcription Exercise 7–5

 **AUDIO 1–57**

Fricative and Affricate Consonants: /ʃ/ʒ/tʃ/dʒ/   Phoneme Study Cards: 13–14, 17–18

1. shoeshine   _____

2. digestion   _____

3. confusion   _____

4. entourage   _____

5. agriculture   _____

6. vivacious   _____

7. sabotage   _____

8. enchanted   _____

9. Jake   _____

10. ship-to-shore   _____

11. stagecoach   _____

12. childish   _____

13. hodgepodge   _____

14. Parisian   _____

15. suggestion   _____

16. chinchilla   _____

17. collection   _____

18. fortunate   _____

19. beautician   _____

20. visualize   _____

STUDY QUESTIONS

1. What symbols combine to form affricates?

_____

_____

2. Affricates are also called:

_____

_____

3. Why are affricates considered obstruents?

_____

_____

4. What is a common articulatory substitution for /tʃ/?

_____

_____

5. List two words that contain the /tʃ/ and /dʒ/ phonemes.

_____

_____

6. Why is it important to have the two components of affricates touch?

_____

_____

CHAPTER

8

Consonants:
Oral Resonants /w/j/l/r/

Learning Objectives

After reading this chapter, you will be able to:

1. Define the term "approximation" and relationship to oral resonant production.

2. State which oral resonant can intrude between two vowels.

3. Describe unique airflow for production of /l/.

4. State how preceding vowels can influence /r/ production.

5. Transcribe words using oral resonant consonants.

Unlike the stop-consonants or fricatives, which are produced with full or partial obstruction of the vocal tract, the /w/j/l/ and /r/ consonants are vowel-like, as the breath stream glides smoothly through the vocal tract. The obstruction that occurs with this group of consonants is caused by *approximation* of the articulators. Approximation is defined as a position of closeness of the articulators.

The /r/ and /l/ phonemes are also referred to as *liquids*. However, most phoneticians view /r/ as a glide. These consonants are termed *oral resonant* due to changes in the oral cavity. These changes result from raising or lowering the mandible, lowering or elevating the tongue, and changing lip opening and rounding of the lips. All of these can change the shape of the oral cavity.

/w/

Transcription Exercise 8–1    AUDIO 1–58

		I	M	F
1.	once			
2.	widow			
3.	Guam			
4.	twice			
5.	iguana			
6.	where			
7.	kiwi			
8.	question			
9.	willow			
10.	anguish			

Transcription Exercise 8–2

 **AUDIO 1–59**

Consonant: /w/

Refer to Study Card: 25

Phonetic Symbol	Target Word	Transcription
/w/	1. wax	
	2. jaguar	
	3. beware	
	4. swell	
	5. wonder	
	6. queen	
	7. forward	
	8. twin	
	9. wet	

/w/

Distinctive Features	Tongue Position
Bilabial lingua-palatal or lingua-velar glide Voiced, back, labial, sonorant, noncontinuant, nonsibilant, nonnasal /W/ →	High back position (as for /u/) Moves into position for following sound. Lips are rounded and protruded, but may unround quickly for transition to next sound.

Voicing/Velopharyngeal Port	Spelling Variations
Voiced—vocal folds *ad*ducted. VP port is closed.	o *one*, *once*, every*o*ne w silent in *who*, *whole*, *sword*, *answer*, *write* /ng/ u /w/ glide occurs for /u/ in language [læŋgwɪdʒ]

Word Positions	Clinical Information
Initial and medial positions in SAE	kw represents the "q" sound as in *quit*. Can be omitted from clusters such as sw in *sweet*.

ORAL RESONANTS

Word Search #10   Answers in Appendix B

```
g   w   ɑ   n   t   ɑ   n   ɑ   m   o   b   e
ʃ   ɛ   w   e   r   s   ð   r   d   b   ʃ   s
s   ɑ   b   s   ð   ŋ   l   r   j   o   m   h
æ   p   v   ɪ   v   o   ʃ   tʃ  b   m   n   aʊ
n   ɑ   k   v   f   w   ɑ   t   ɚ   l   u   w
w   p   r   ɪ   i   ʌ   ə   j   v   w   θ   ɪ
ɑ   w   ɝ   l   d   w   ɔ   r   w   ʌ   n   t
n   tʃ  ɪ   w   p   b   t   d   k   g   s   z
h   ɑ   b   ɔ   r   æ   p   e   p   k   w   ɚ
ɪ   ʒ   n   r   e   dʒ  ɚ   u   ɔ   o   θ   o
l   ʃ   æ   ʊ   t   b   n   z   b   l   ɑ   ð
r   w   ɛ   p   ə   n   e   w   l   d   j   ɝ
d   p   ɛ   t   e   v   i   h   b   w   e   m
p   æ   n   d   p   aʊ  w   ɚ   ʊ   ɔ   l   u
ɚ   z   d   ɔ   l   t   r   d   ʒ   r   v   i
```

Directions: Find and circle the words listed below which contain the /w/ phoneme.

Civil War	howitzer
World War One	Cold War
Guantanamo Bay	power
Waterloo	weapon

/j/

Transcription Exercise 8–3

 AUDIO 1–60

		I	M	F
1.	inject			
2.	royal			
3.	yet			
4.	zillion			
5.	bunion			
6.	spaniel			
7.	yoyo			
8.	layette			
9.	figure			
10.	coyote			

Transcription Exercise 8–4

Consonant: /j/

🔊 **AUDIO 1–61**

Refer to Study Card: 23

Phonetic Symbol	Target Word	Transcription
/j/	1. your	
	2. beyond	
	3. yield	
	4. papaya	
	5. yonder	
	6. familiar	
	7. yarn	
	8. billion	
	9. yes	

/j/

Distinctive Features	Tongue Position
Lingua-palatal glide Voiced, back, nonlabial, sonorant, noncontinuant, nonsibilant, non-nasal ←— /j/	Tongue is in high front position, approximating /i/ and is ready to move into position for the next sound.

Voicing/Velopharyngeal Port	Spelling Variations
Voiced—vocal folds *ad*duct. VP port is closed.	i on*i*on, Will*i*am j hallelu*j*ah l bouil*l*on /j/ is often intrusive between words ending in /i/ or /ɪ/ and those beginning with a vowel: see it [sijɪt]

Word Positions	Clinical Information
Initial and medial positions in SAE	Articulation error: substituted with /w/ or omitted

/l/

Transcription Exercise 8–5   🔊 **AUDIO 1–62**

		I	M	F
1.	mall			
2.	linoleum			
3.	whale			
4.	apple			
5.	fellow			
6.	calves			
7.	lullaby			
8.	flotilla			
9.	helm			
10.	sociable			

Transcription Exercise 8–6

Consonant: /l/

🔊 AUDIO 1–63

Refer to Study Card: 22

Phonetic Symbol	Target Word	Transcription
/l/	1. lucky	
	2. lemon	
	3. clown	
	4. sandal	
	5. golden	
	6. else	
	7. bridal	
	8. flea	
	9. Leon	

/l/

Distinctive Features	Tongue Position
Lingua-alveolar lateral (liquid) Voiced, front, nonlabial, sonorant, noncontinuant, nonsibilant, nonnasal /l/ ⟶	Tip of tongue and part of blade contact upper alveolar ridge. Lips are apart and neutral. Airflow is around the sides of the tongue for lateral emission of airstream.

Voicing/Velopharyngeal Port	Spelling Variations
Voiced—vocal folds *ad*duct. VP port is closed.	Appears consistently as *l* le bott*le*, midd*le* el funn*el*, kenn*el* sl with silent *s* in ai*sle*

Word Positions	Clinical Information
Initial, medial, and final positions in SAE	This phoneme's unique feature is the airflow around the *sides* of the tongue.

/r/

Transcription Exercise 8–7

🔊 AUDIO 1–64

		I	M	F
1.	wrap			
2.	rye			
3.	scar			
4.	report			
5.	rubber			
6.	wardrobe			
7.	wry			
8.	garden			
9.	before			
10.	deer			

Transcription Exercise 8–8

◀))) **AUDIO 1–65**

Consonant: /r/

Refer to Study Card: 24

Phonetic Symbol	Target Word	Transcription
/r/	1. write	
	2. impress	
	3. reduce	
	4. sorry	
	5. rhyme	
	6. already	
	7. chair	
	8. rub	
	9. bar	

/r/

Distinctive Features	Tongue Position
Alveo-palatal liquid (glide) Voiced, front, labial, sonorant, noncontinuant, nonsibilant, nonnasal ← —/r/	Sides of the tongue are against upper molars. Back of tongue may be slightly elevated. Front of tongue usually is in close approximation to alveolar ridge. Retroflex position: Produced as above but tongue tip curls up and back. Lips may be slightly protruded similar to /ʊ/ but usually take the position of the surrounding vowel. If tongue tip is curled back toward palate, referred to as retroflex.

Voicing/Velopharyngeal Port	Spelling Variations
Voiced—vocal folds *ad*duct. VP port is closed.	wr *wrote*, *wren* rh *rhinoceros*, *rhyme*

Word Positions	Clinical Information
Initial, medial, and final positions in SAE	Common articulation error is substitution of w/r, especially in children under the age of 7 years. The IPA cites /ɹ/, but phoneticians in the U.S.A. use /r/.

Influence of the /r/ Sound

The /r/ phoneme can influence the vowel that precedes it. The vowels /i/ɛ/ɑ/o/ can occur with the /r/ in the same syllable as in the words "deer" [dir], "care" [kɛr], "star" [stɑr], and "more" [mor].

The influence of the /r/ sound occurs especially in the vowel + r combination of /ɛr/, as in the word "hair" [hɛr]. Because of the location of the vowel adjacent to the /r/, the front of the tongue is in a lower position than would normally be expected. In this way, the tongue position makes the vowel sound of the /e/ closer to that of /ɛ/, resulting in the use of /ɛr/.

/ir/

 **AUDIO 1–66**

		I	M	F
1.	spear			
2.	weird			
3.	series			
4.	steer			
5.	pear			
6.	fierce			
7.	era			
8.	career			
9.	mirth			
10.	wire			

/ɛr/

Transcription Exercise 8–10   🔊 **AUDIO 1–67**

		I	M	F
1.	stair			
2.	square			
3.	barrel			
4.	ware			
5.	trailer			
6.	stare			
7.	pearl			
8.	chair			
9.	bear			
10.	caramel			

/ɑr/

Transcription Exercise 8–11   🔊 **AUDIO 1–68**

		I	M	F
1.	heart			
2.	star			
3.	sergeant			
4.	farce			
5.	carriage			
6.	stare			
7.	marry			
8.	marine			
9.	party			
10.	carbon			

/or/

Transcription Exercise 8–12

🔊 **AUDIO 1–69**

		I	M	F
1.	fourth			
2.	quart			
3.	parlor			
4.	wharf			
5.	soar			
6.	wart			
7.	rumor			
8.	court			
9.	pour			
10.	world			

VOWEL +r

Answers in Appendix B

t	n	ʒ	g	f	o	r	s	k	o	r	m
k	p	s	ʃ	j	s	g	o	v	f	o	e
e	z	ə	ɪ	ʌ	j	i	r	l	i	ʒ	o
k	n	ɛ	u	g	ɑ	r	d	b	z	ɔ	f
r	ks	o	j	i	t	θ	h	m	θ	ʊ	i
ɛ	r	f	ɛ	r	r	d	f	m	ɚ	i	r
f	o	r	w	o	r	n	w	ɑ	ʌ	ɪ	s
b	g	k	ɛ	r	w	r	o	r	n	ɛ	p
u	s	r	p	e	ɚ	i	r	ʃ	ə	ð	b
l	k	tʃ	k	ɑ	r	f	ɛ	r	h	e	t
k	w	j	d	r	s	z	s	l	ɛ	d	d
ɛ	ɛ	z	s	n	m	ɑ	ŋ	dʒ	z	ɛ	k
ə	r	z	ɚ	k	o	r	t	j	ɑ	r	d
r	g	ʊ	p	o	r	z	ʊ	w	o	i	g

Directions: Find and circle the words listed below that contain the vowel + r sounds: /ir/or/ɑr/ɛr/.

yearly	guard	czars	dairy	forewarn
sword	square	carfare	pours	
ear	marsh	airfare	fourscore	
gear	fierce	careworn	courtyard	

Crossword Puzzle for /j/, /l/, and /r/

Answers in Appendix B

Directions: Transcribe the following words:

Across:
2. yellow
4. rose
5. jungle green
7. violet
8. maroon

Down:
1. teal
3. orange
6. lavender

WHAT'S IN A NAME?

Word Search #12

Answers in Appendix B

r u θ v g e h k o w k l

s ə s ɪ o k ɑ l i n m o

ɪ n s ɑ g n j u k r v r

l r r ə b m ŋ i o ɚ ɛ ɛ

ɛ ə u f l o t z θ ʌ s t

r l d r ə s ə l l ɛ o ə

i d ɑ m t j o h æ n r ɚ

s f f r ɑ n ə l d ʃ t i

o p ks k d e r u ð s m l

l o r e n e f ə t s r e

t t dʒ g g ʃ o ʊ b j ɛ n

m ɪ o l ɪ v i ə tʃ ɛ t ð

r h r z ʒ ð c ɑ ɪ t k o

e h j o l æ n d ə ɑ w ə

Directions: Find and circle the words listed below that contain the /j/, /l/, or /r/ phonemes.

Rudolph	Ronald	Ruth
Yolanda	Louise	Colleen
Russell	Johann	Elaine
Olivia	Loretta	Yetta
Lorraine	Larry	Rebecca

Transcription Exercise 8–13

Vowel + r: /or/ir/ɛr/ɑr/

1. earmark _____

2. careworn _____

3. ore _____

4. spears _____

5. carport _____

6. sheer _____

7. hardware _____

8. dart _____

9. forlorn _____

10. rare _____

11. sparse _____

12. aardvark _____

13. jeer _____

14. bore _____

15. foursquare _____

16. farce _____

17. coarse _____

18. smears _____

19. starch _____

20. bear _____

Transcription Exercise 8–14

Oral Resonant Consonants: /l/r/j/w/

1. yoke _____

2. dwarf _____

3. leeway _____

4. dominion _____

5. quibble _____

6. larceny _____

7. uranium _____

8. illustrate _____

9. rally _____

10. Sawyer _____

11. radiator _____

12. quietly _____

13. valiant _____

14. frequency _____

15. lawyer _____

16. wayward _____

17. Yolanda _____

18. stallions _____

19. wrestle _____

20. yawn _____

STUDY QUESTIONS

1. What is the source of oral cavity obstruction when an oral resonant is produced?

   _____

   _____

2. What is the phonetic context for intrusion of /j/?

   _____

   _____

3. What consonant combination represents "q"?

   _____

   _____

4. What is unique in production of /l/?

   _____

   _____

5. List five words that contain /r/.

   _____

   _____

6. Define *approximation*.

   _____

   _____

CHAPTER

9

Articulation of Vowels

Learning Objectives

After reading this chapter, you will be able to:

1. Define "vowel."

2. State the importance of the use of Vowel Quadrangle for identifying vowel position.

3. Identify horizontal and vertical tongue reference points used in the Vowel Quadrangle.

4. Explain the tongue position for tense and lax vowels.

Vowels play a very special role in our speech by forming the nucleus of a fundamental unit of phonetic structure: the syllable. Syllables are discussed in Chapter 2. Production of vowels differs from consonant production because the tongue does not make contact with a specific articulator for closure. Unlike consonants, vowels are produced with a mostly unobstructed vocal tract. In contrast to consonants, vowels are classified solely by tongue placement to describe *place* of articulation. All vowels are voiced.

Simple vowels are also termed *monophthongs* (defined as *single* sounds). Monophthongs comprise most of the American English vowel system (Lowe & Blosser, 2002).

Diphthongs (defined as *two* sounds) require two articulatory positions, as they are produced by rapid gliding from one vowel to another vowel position. Because vowels and diphthongs are required to form a syllable, they are also termed *syllabics*.

Prominent Articulatory Vowel Positions

The vowel quadrangle (Figure 9–1) is a useful tool to describe vowel production as it provides convenient reference points for specifying tongue position.

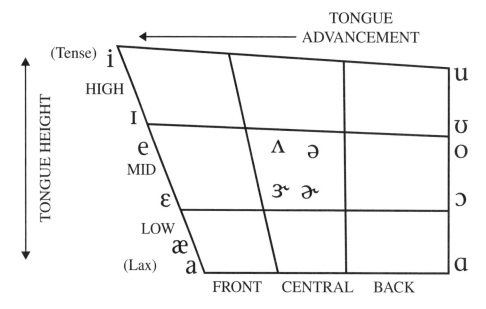

Figure 9–1. The vowel quadrangle.

The position of the *highest point of the arch of the tongue* is considered to be the point of articulation of the vowel. The *vertical dimension* of the vowel quadrangle is known as vowel *height*: high, central (mid), or low. The *horizontal dimension* of the vowel quadrangle, or tongue advancement, identifies how far forward the tongue is located in the oral cavity.

Vowels are also described by the tenseness or laxness of the tongue. A tense vowel requires muscular tension at the root of the tongue. The tongue is elevated and tense for production of the /i/u/e/ vowels. Lax vowels require less muscular tension at the root of the tongue, such as /a/æ/ɚ/. These vowels are produced by a low tongue position in the oral cavity.

After you have studied this chapter and have learned the sound/symbol relationship of vowels, take a movie break and watch *My Fair Lady* (1964). During the movie, you will hear Dr. Peter Ladefoged, who was director of the UCLA Phonetics Laboratory, produce vowel sounds as Dr. Henry Higgins (Rex Harrison) is trying to change Eliza Doolittle's Cockney dialect. Dr. Ladefoged, a pioneer in the field of phonetics, died in 2007.

STUDY QUESTIONS

1. What speech role do vowels play in forming syllables?

   Vowels form the nucleus of a fundamental unit of phonetic structure: the syllable

2. How does production of vowels differ from consonants?

   The tongue does not make contact with a specific articulator for closure

3. What is the configuration of the vocal tract used for production of vowels?

   Mostly unobstructed vocal tract

4. What is difference between monophthongs and diphthongs?

   monophthongs: simple vowels, single sounds
   diphthongs: 2 sounds; glide from 1 vowel to the next
   & 2 articulatory positions

5. What does vowel quadrangle provide that is helpful for identifying vowel production?

   reference points that specify tongue positions

6. What do vertical and horizontal dimensions of the vowel quadrangle indicate for tongue position?

   vertical position represents vowel height
   horizontal position represents how far forward the tongue is located in the oral cavity

7. What is the difference between a tense and lax tongue?

   tense: requires muscular tension at the root of the tongue lax: requires less muscular tension at the root of the tongue

10

Front Vowels

Learning Objectives

After reading this chapter, you will be able to:

1. Explain where front vowels are produced in the oral cavity.

2. List spelling variations for front vowels.

3. State lip position for front vowels.

4. Transcribe words using front vowels.

As the name implies, front vowels of Standard American English are produced in the front of the oral cavity. The tongue is shifted forward to produce /i/ɪ/e/ɛ/æ/. As you say these vowels, you will note that your tongue begins at the highest point in the oral cavity and progresses downward to the lowest point. These vowels are produced with unrounded lips that may be slightly retracted. Some phoneticians include the capped "a" /a/ (used in diphthongs) as a low front vowel.

/i/

Transcription Exercise 10–1 🔊 **AUDIO 2–1**

		I	M	F
1.	yes			
2.	leaving			
3.	eel			
4.	thieves			
5.	people			
6.	cheapen			
7.	quiche			
8.	street			
9.	helix			
10.	hire			

Transcription Exercise 10–2

🔊 **AUDIO 2–2**

Vowel: /i/

Refer to Study Card: 26

Phonetic Symbol	Target Word	Transcription
/i/	1. eat	/it/
	2. keep	/kip/
	3. deed	/did/
	4. key	
	5. beak	
	6. peak	
	7. beet	
	8. tea	
	9. deep	

/i/

Distinctive Features	Tongue Position
High front tense (unrounded) vowel	Tongue moves forward and elevates toward hard palate.
	Sides of back of tongue close against upper molars.
	Front portion of tongue is raised high in oral cavity.
	Lips are parted slightly.
	Airflow is through the oral cavity.

/i/ →

Voicing/Velopharyngeal Port	Spelling Variations
Voiced—vocal folds *ad*duct.	e be, me, we
VP port is closed.	ee feet, three
	ea eat, teach, east
	ey key

Word Positions	Clinical Information
Initial, medial, and final positions in SAE	

/ɪ/

Transcription Exercise 10–3 ◀))) AUDIO 2–3

		I	M	F
1.	mild			
2.	it			
3.	pixie			
4.	billion			
5.	fine			
6.	guilt			
7.	villain			
8.	sincere			
9.	lymph			
10.	fin			

Transcription Exercise 10–4

Vowel: /ɪ/

🔊)) **AUDIO 2–4**

Refer to Study Card: 27

Phonetic Symbol	Target Word	Transcription
/ɪ/	1. kick	/KIK/
	2. gig	/gɪg/
	3. build	/bɪld/
	4. tick	
	5. it	
	6. bit	
	7. pick	
	8. kid	
	9. big	

/ɪ/

Distinctive Features	Tongue Position
High front lax (unrounded) vowel 	Middle to front portion of tongue is raised toward hard palate and alveolar ridge. Sides of back of tongue close against upper molars. Tip of tongue touches lightly behind lower front teeth. Lips are apart. Airflow is through the oral cavity.

Voicing/Velopharyngeal Port	Spelling Variations
Voiced—vocal folds *ad*duct. VP port is closed.	i *if, in* y *gy*m, *hy*mn ee b*ee*n ui q*ui*z o w*o*men u b*u*sy

Word Position	Clinical Information
Initial, medial, and final positions in SAE	Referred to as the "short i" Many prefer to transcribe using /i/ rather than /ɪ/ in syllables that are unstressed as in "baby" ['bebi].

/ε/

Transcription Exercise 10–5

🔊)) AUDIO 2–5

		I	M	F
1.	entail			
2.	penguin			
3.	bell			
4.	mild			
5.	yes			
6.	elf			
7.	gang			
8.	ethic			
9.	guess			
10.	jealous			

Note: The /ε/ is frequently substituted with /ɪ/ in Standard American English dialects:

"get" [gεt] [gɪt]
"pen" [pεn] [pɪn]

Transcription Exercise 10–6

Vowel: /ɛ/

🔊 **AUDIO 2–6**

Refer to Study Card: 28

Phonetic Symbol	Target Word	Transcription
/ɛ/	1. meld	/mɛld/
	2. end	/ɛnd/
	3. dell	/dɛl/
	4. den	
	5. led	
	6. knell	
	7. dense	
	8. sled	
	9. etch	

/ɛ/

Distinctive Features	Tongue Position
Mid-front lax (unrounded) vowel /ɛ/ ⟶	Sides of back of tongue touch against upper molars. Middle to front portion of tongue is raised slightly toward hard palate and alveolar ridge. Tip of tongue touches lightly behind lower front teeth. Lips are apart and neutral. Airflow is through the oral cavity.

Voicing/Velopharyngeal Port	Spelling Variations
Voiced—vocal folds *ad*duct. VP port is closed.	e *end, ebb, ten* ea *head, steady* ai *said* ie *friend*

Word Positions	Clinical Information
Initial and medial positions in SAE	Also known as the epsilon (from the Greek alphabet) or "short e"

/e/

Transcription Exercise 10–7

		I	M	F
1.	acorn			
2.	sleigh			
3.	vein			
4.	dial			
5.	leisure			
6.	gain			
7.	bag			
8.	lei			
9.	attain			
10.	reindeer			

Transcription Exercise 10–8

Vowel: /e/

🔊 **AUDIO 2–8**

Refer to Study Card: 29

Phonetic Symbol	Target Word	Transcription
/e/ √ X	1. vase	/ v e ɪ s /
√ X	2. stays	/ s t e ɪ z /
√ X	3. Zane	/ z e ɪ n /
	4. ate	
	5. faze	
	6. taste	
	7. face	
	8. shave	
	9. fate	

1. ves , vez , vaz (It depends on how you say it)
2. stez
3. zen

You can use phoneme /e/ or
diphthong ēɪ /eɪ/
Both are acceptable

/e/

Distinctive Features	Tongue Position
Mid-front tense (unrounded) vowel	Tongue is raised to mid-portion of oral cavity and shifts forward. Tip is at lower front teeth and makes contact with posterior portion of alveolar ridge; tongue contacts upper molars laterally. Lips are apart. Airflow is through the oral cavity.

Voicing/Velopharyngeal Port	Spelling Variations
Voiced—vocal folds *ad*duct. VP port is closed.	a *a*che et ball*et* ea st*ea*k ai g*ai*t ee matin*ee*

Word Position	Clinical Information
Initial, medial, and final positions in SAE	Also known as the "long a" Some phoneticians use /eɪ/ to represent this sound.

/æ/

Transcription Exercise 10–9

 **AUDIO 2–9**

		I	M	F
1.	advance			
2.	pan			
3.	ant			
4.	mall			
5.	pain			
6.	dampness			
7.	quack			
8.	cascade			
9.	math			
10.	went			

Transcription Exercise 10–10

Vowel: /æ/

🔊 **AUDIO 2–10**

Refer to Study Card: 30

Phonetic Symbol	Target Word	Transcription
/æ/	1. sash	/sæʃ/
	2. fast	/fæst/
	3. ash	/æʃ/
	4. staff	
	5. vat	
	6. shaft	
	7. tat	
	8. as	
	9. salve	

/æ/

Distinctive Features	Tongue Position
Low front lax (unrounded) vowel /æ/ ⟶	Middle to front portion of tongue is raised toward hard palate, but is low in the mouth so that it rarely contacts upper molars. Tip of tongue is near lower front teeth. Lips are widely separated. Airflow is through the oral cavity. Of all the front vowels, the mandible is in the lowest position.
Voicing/Velopharyngeal Port	**Spelling Variations**
Voiced—vocal folds *ad*duct. VP port is closed.	a *a*t ai pl*ai*d ua g*ua*rantee au l*au*gh i mer*i*ngue
Word Positions	**Clinical Information**
Initial and medial positions in SAE	Also known as "short a" or "ash"

Crossword Puzzle for /i/, /ɪ/, /ɛ/, /æ/, /e/, and /w/

Answers in Appendix B

Directions: Transcribe the following words:

Across:
1. Webster
2. Winston
4. Lane
5. Mary

Down:
1. Wynn
2. William
3. Tim
6. Sheila

FOR THE BIRDS

Word Search #13   Answers in Appendix B

v	g	e	h	k	g	r	i	b	o	w	k
f	ɪ	n	p	i	k	ɑ	k	z	v	m	z
l	i	p	w	ʌ	tʃ	ɪ	k	ə	b	i	ɔ
o	g	ɛ	ʃ	b	ə	l	d	f	ɛ	v	u
t	ə	r	o	m	s	e	ɛ	g	s	g	r
p	l	ə	ɛ	t	f	g	n	d	o	ə	k
i	ð	k	ɚ	l	æ	k	d	v	r	ʃ	i
r	ɝ	i	ʌ	b	l	u	dʒ	e	t	j	w
ɛ	r	t	θ	k	k	dʒ	s	r	m	ɚ	i
n	i	n	n	æ	ə	tʃ	ɪ	t	æ	ɛ	s
ɔ	n	g	m	o	n	n	ə	w	g	ə	f
ʒ	e	r	l	j	h	e	ɛ	ð	p	t	ɪ
h	i	g	r	ɛ	t	z	d	r	aɪ	ŋ	n
m	ɪ	o	l	ɪ	t	v	i	ə	i	i	tʃ

Directions: Find and circle the words listed below that contain the front vowels: /i/ɪ/ɛ/æ/e/.

eagle	finch	grebe
egg	parakeet	chickadee
blue jay	egret	kiwi
wren	eaglet	peacock
falcon	canary	

Transcription Exercise 10–11

Front Vowels: /i/ɪ/ɛ/e/æ/

1. flame   /fleɪm/

2. alley   /æli/

3. believe   /bɪliv/

4. raisin   /reɪzɪn/

5. weekday   /wikdeɪ/

6. relax   _____

7. ask   _____

8. people   _____

9. remnant   _____

10. reign   _____

11. gymnast   _____

12. apron   _____

13. namesake _____

14. busy   _____

15. caffeine _____

16. women   _____

17. headache _____

18. please   _____

19. biscuit   _____

20. eldest   _____

bəliv
biliv   } depends on
bɪliv   } how you say it

STUDY QUESTIONS

1. What is lip position for front vowels?

   _____

   _____

2. /ɪ/ is also referred to as:

   _____

   _____

3. What vowel is known as "short a"?

   _____

   _____

4. List three spelling variations for /ɪ/.

   _____

   _____

5. For what front vowel is the mandible in the lowest position of all front vowels?

   _____

   _____

6. What front vowel is identified as the "short e"?

   _____

   _____

7. What diphthong do some phoneticians use for /e/?

   _____

   _____

11

Central Vowels

Learning Objectives

After reading this chapter, you will be able to:

1. State the use of central vowels in stressed syllables in words.

2. Explain the three ways production of /ɝ/ and /r/ differ.

3. Transcribe /ɝ/ and /ʌ/ contrast words.

4. Identify vowel reduction in words for use of the schwa.

5. Transcribe words using central vowels.

The central vowels are /ə/ʌ/ɚ/ɝ/. As the name indicates, these vowels are produced in the middle (central) portion of the oral cavity, midway between the front and back vowels. The /ə/ and /ɚ/ are classified as unstressed vowels. They are used in unstressed syllables and produced with less force. The /ʌ/ and /ɝ/ are used in stressed syllables and produced with more force.

The /ɚ/ and /ɝ/ are also referred to as rhotacized, or r-colored vowels, due to the influence of the /r/ sound. Garn-Nunn and Lynn (2004) state that the /ɝ/ and /r/ differ in these ways: (1) /ɝ/ produced with greater duration, (2) /ɝ/ can form a syllable, (3) tongue moves toward the /r/ consonant production, and (4) unlike /ɝ/, /r/ is voiceless following a voiceless consonant.

This category of vowels is usually difficult for beginning phonetics students to master because it can be difficult to determine whether a stressed or unstressed vowel should be used. Indeed, even seasoned phoneticians may have difficulty transcribing these vowels consistently. Edwards (2003) reports that some phoneticians in America use only the unstressed central vowels (/ə/ɚ/). However, in the study of phonetics, it is important to learn the use of the central vowels. Transcription Exercises 11–10 through 11–15 provide extra central vowel transcription practice.

/ə/

Transcription Exercise 11–1

 **AUDIO 2–12**

		I	M	F
1.	ahead			
2.	rattan			
3.	machine			
4.	baton			
5.	cabana			
6.	tuba			
7.	vanilla			
8.	agree			
9.	buffet			
10.	cocoon			

Transcription Exercise 11–2

🔊 **AUDIO 2–13**

Vowel: /ə/

Refer to Study Card: 31

Phonetic Symbol	Target Word	Transcription
/ə/	1. galore	/ gəlɔr /
	2. support	/səpɔrt/
	3. alone	/ əloʊn/
	4. compose	
	5. condone	
	6. patrol	
	7. rapport	
	8. ashore	
	9. lagoon	

· o or oʊ
1) acceptable

/ə/

Distinctive Features	Tongue Position
Midcentral lax vowel (unrounded, unstressed)	Tongue is flat, but can have a slight arch; tip is at lower front teeth.
	Lips are apart and neutral.
	Airflow is through the oral cavity.

Voicing/Velopharyngeal Port	Spelling Variations
Voiced—vocal folds *ad*duct.	There is no specific letter of the alphabet to represent the schwa. Can substitute for any vowel:
VP port is closed.	a m*a*chine
	u talc*u*m
	e r*e*port
	i hosp*i*tal
	o pr*o*found
	ai uncert*ai*n
	eo pig*eo*n

Word Positions	Clinical Information
Initial, medial, and final positions in SAE	Known as the schwa

Crossword Puzzle for /ə/

Answers in Appendix B

Directions: Transcribe the following words:

Across:
4. suppose
5. cocoon
6. lagoon

Down:
1. papoose
2. guzzle
3. upon

/ʌ/

Transcription Exercise 11–3  **AUDIO 2–14**

		I	M	F
1.	of			
2.	chug			
3.	won			
4.	uncut			
5.	was			
6.	young			
7.	rust			
8.	up			
9.	one			
10.	roost			

Transcription Exercise 11–4

🔊)) **AUDIO 2–15**

Vowel: /ʌ/

Refer to Study Card: 32

Phonetic Symbol	Target Word	Transcription
/ʌ/	1. oven	/ʌvən/
	2. touch	/tʌtʃ/
	3. thumb	/θʌm/
	4. bum	
	5. ton	
	6. pun	
	7. mutt	
	8. cud	
	9. nut	

ʌvɪn or ʌvən
are acceptable
(uh-vin; uh-ven)

/ʌ/

Distinctive Features	Tongue Position
Midcentral vowel (unrounded, stressed)	See tongue position for schwa /ə/
	Tongue may be slightly more retracted as in production for /ɑ/.
	Produced with more muscular tension of the tongue than /ə/.

Voicing/Velopharyngeal Port	Spelling Variations
Voiced—vocal folds *ad*duct. VP port is closed.	u most frequent and consistent as in p*u*g, s*u*n, h*u*ndred ou r*ou*gh, d*ou*ble o t*o*n, s*o*n, t*o*ngue oe d*oe*s oo bl*oo*d

Word Positions	Clinical Information
Initial and medial positions in SAE	Also referred to as the caret or inverted "v."

Note. The /ʌ/ is used in the popular expression "duh" [dʌ]. Question: Is learning phonetics challenging? Answer: Duh! Or, remember the beginning sounds of the theme to the movie *Jaws* (1975): "duh-duhn . . ."

Crossword Puzzle for /ʌ/

Answers in Appendix B

Directions: Transcribe the following words:

Across:
3. unglued
6. shut

Down:
1. dust
2. hush
4. gumbo
5. duck

/ɚ/

Transcription Exercise 11–5   🔊 AUDIO 2–16

		I	M	F
1.	actor			
2.	earner			
3.	nerd			
4.	sugar			
5.	anger			
6.	neighbor			
7.	creature			
8.	curtain			
9.	glamour			
10.	paper			

Transcription Exercise 11–6

🔊 **AUDIO 2–17**

Vowel: /ɚ/

Refer to Study Card: 33

Phonetic Symbol	Target Word	Transcription
/ɚ/	1. nature	/ˈneɪtʃɚ/ ɚ ɝ
	2. major	/ˈmeɪdʒɚ/
	3. baker	/ˈbeɪkɚ/
	4. razor	
	5. later	
	6. pacer	
	7. failure	
	8. neighbor	
	9. safer	

ɚ = unstressed syllables

/ˈneɪtʃɚ/   ər → ɚ or ɝ

/ɚ/

Distinctive Features	Tongue Position
Midcentral r-colored lax vowel (unstressed) 	Tongue is slightly elevated from neutral position. Sides of tongue close against upper molars. Lips are apart. Airflow is through the oral cavity. Produced with same tongue position as /ɝ/ with the exception that the tongue is more relaxed and duration of this phoneme is shorter than for /ɝ/.

Voicing/Velopharyngeal Port	Spelling Variations
Voiced—vocal folds *ad*duct. VP port is closed.	Most often used in unstressed positions of words: er butt*er* or maj*or* our glam*our* ur *Saturday* ure meas*ure*

Word Positions	Clinical Information
Initial, medial, and final positions in SAE	Also known as the hooked schwar or unstressed schwar.

Crossword Puzzle for /ɚ/

Answers in Appendix B

Directions: Transcribe the following words:

Across:
3. flower
4. lantern

Down:
1. ever
2. effort
4. leader
5. never

/ɝ/

Transcription Exercise 11–7    **AUDIO 2–18**

		I	M	F
1.	herb			
2.	worst			
3.	slur			
4.	chirp			
5.	surgeon			
6.	urn			
7.	purchase			
8.	earn			
9.	turtle			
10.	myrtle			

Transcription Exercise 11–8

Vowel: /ɝ/

Refer to Study Card: 34

Phonetic Symbol	Target Word	Transcription
/ɝ/ X	1. urge	/ ɝdʒ /
X	2. verb	/ vɝb /
X	3. birth	/ bɝθ /
	4. third	
	5. dirge	
	6. burr	
	7. girth	
	8. germ	
	9. earth	

1. ɝdʒ

2. vɝb

3. bɝθ

/ɝ/

Distinctive Features	Tongue Position
Midcentral r-colored tense vowel (stressed)	Tongue is slightly elevated from neutral position.
	Sides of tongue close against upper molars.
	Lips are apart.
	Airflow is through the oral cavity.

Voicing/Velopharyngeal Port	Spelling Variations
Voiced—vocal folds *ad*duct.	er h*er*d, m*er*chant, f*er*n
VP port is closed.	ur *ur*ge, f*ur*, t*ur*tle
	ir ch*ir*p, b*ir*th
	ear *ear*n, p*ear*l
	or w*or*m
	our j*our*ney

Word Positions	Clinical Information
Initial, medial, and final positions in SAE	Also known as the reversed, hooked epsilon, and stressed schwar.

Crossword Puzzle for /ɝ/

Answers in Appendix B

	1		
	2		

Directions: Transcribe the following words:

Across:
2. herbal
4. thirsty
6. nursemaid

Down:
1. burst
3. zircon
5. third

MIDCENTRAL VOWELS

Word Search #14   Answers in Appendix B

k p s ɝ θ k i o s ɪ l v ɚ s

r e o z n n p f ɛ l b z ɛ t

ɛ ʌ ð p ɛ d b ɝ t i w ɝ f o

k b e h w j r dʒ i d e dʒ ɚ θ

ɚ s h ɝ ɑ p j z θ ɚ ʌ ʊ t h

d b ʌ l h m e u ɝ ʍ ɝ ɛ u dʒ

p s f i ə p m p v n θ p ɝ ə

n æ ɪ ɚ n m ɛ d ɚ m ʍ t ð ʌ

d h n o dʒ n ʍ t æ ŋ e t o h

e ʃ ɝ t v g s o n æ k d ʃ æ

m w s θ s t p h ɑ g ɚ o g m

m j p v t v ɝ ʌ d ɚ z t m ə

g t i z o t s f n ɛ w tʃ e h

t v w ɛ j r w m ɑ d ɚ n dʒ o

Directions: Find and circle the words listed below that contain the /ɝ/or /ɚ/ phonemes.

earthquake	nurse	record
urge	modern	effort
earlier	paper	hammer
purse	leader	
shirt	silver	

Transcription Exercise 11–9

Central Vowels: /ə/ʌ/ɚ/ɝ/

🔊 **AUDIO 2–20**

Phoneme Study Cards: 31–34

1. hamburger   _____

2. suds   _____

3. kern   _____

4. cover   _____

5. occur   _____

6. fervor   _____

7. undone   _____

8. eardrum   _____

9. murmur   _____

10. awhile   _____

11. turner   _____

12. confirm   _____

13. buzzer   _____

14. mature   _____

15. buffer   _____

16. chirp   _____

17. serge   _____

18. verse   _____

19. submerge   _____

20. merger   _____

Transcription Exercise 11–10    **AUDIO 2–21**

To help you become familiar with the sound of the schwa /ə/, listen to these words and the transcription. All of these words could be articulated with a different vowel rather than the schwa. For example: "famous" could be transcribed as [femɪs] or [femɛs].

Word	Transcription
1. adore	[əˈdor]
2. often	[ˈaftən]
3. committee	[kəˈmɪti]
4. again	[əˈgɛn]
5. famous	[ˈfeməs]
6. balloon	[bəˈlun]
7. possess	[pəˈzɛs]
8. chagrin	[ʃəˈgrɪn]
9. lapel	[ləˈpɛl]
10. regime	[rəˈʒim]

Transcription Exercise 11–11    **AUDIO 2–22**

Where is the schwa? Listen to these words and decide which vowel has been reduced to the schwa. Remember that the schwa can substitute for any vowel. Answers in Appendix B.

1. cousin   _____   _____

2. illness   _____   _____

3. distant   _____   _____

4. promise   _____   _____

5. palace   _____   _____

6. socket   _____   _____

7. disease   _____   _____

8. escape   _____   _____

9. contain   _____   _____

10. divide   _____   _____

Transcription Exercise 11–12

 **AUDIO 2–23**

Central Vowel Stressed Dictation /ʌ/.

Listen and transcribe these words. Answers in Appendix B.

1. gulf   _____

2. dust   _____

3. dumb   _____

4. fuzz   _____

5. putt   _____

6. plus   _____

7. lug   _____

8. stuck   _____

9. crumb   _____

10. plum   _____

Transcription Exercise 11–13

 AUDIO 2–24

Central Vowel Stressed Dictation /ɝ/.

Listen and transcribe these words. Answers in Appendix B.

1. clerk   _____

2. first   _____

3. heard   _____

4. fur   _____

5. cursed   _____

6. shirk   _____

7. were   _____

8. whirl   _____

9. per   _____

10. curl   _____

Transcription Exercise 11–14

 **AUDIO 2–25**

Listen and transcribe these words that contrast central stressed vowels /ʌ/ and /ɝ/. Answers in Appendix B.

1. bun _____   burn _____

2. shuck _____   shirk _____

3. buzz _____   burns _____

4. hut _____   hurt _____

5. shut _____   shirt _____

6. cut _____   curt _____

7. luck _____   lurk _____

8. putt _____   pert _____

9. bust _____   burst _____

10. hub _____   Herb _____

Transcription Exercise 11–15

 **AUDIO 2–26**

Listen and transcribe these words that contain the unstressed central vowel /ɚ/. Answers in Appendix B.

1. plumber   _____

2. other   _____

3. cluster   _____

4. ulcer   _____

5. buffer   _____

6. butler   _____

7. plunger   _____

8. rubber   _____

9. southern   _____

10. sculpture   _____

STUDY QUESTIONS

1. What central vowels are also referred to as rhotacized, or r-colored?

_____

_____

2. Where in oral cavity are central vowels produced?

_____

_____

3. List four ways /ɝ/ and r differ.

_____

_____

4. The schwa is also referred to as:

_____

_____

5. What popular expression is /ʌ/ used in?

_____

_____

6. What central vowel is also referred to as hooked schwar or unstressed schwar?

_____

_____

7. Is /ʌ/ used in stressed or unstressed syllables?

_____

_____

CHAPTER

12

Back Vowels

Learning Objectives

After reading this chapter, you will be able to:

1. State the tongue position for all back vowels and how they are produced.

2. Identify the lip position for back vowels.

3. List the spelling variations for back vowels.

4. Transcribe words using back vowels.

As the name indicates, the back vowels /u/ʊ/o/ɔ/ɑ/ are produced in the back portion of the oral cavity. The posterior portion of the tongue is elevated toward the velum. The tongue tip is behind the lower central incisors, or may lightly touch the lower alveolar ridge. The /ɑ/ has the greatest mandibular opening of all American English-vowel sounds (Garn-Nunn & Lynn, 2004). With the exception of /ɑ/, the lips round or slightly protrude for production of the back vowels.

/u/

Transcription Exercise 12–1   🔊 AUDIO 2–27

		I	M	F
1.	noodle			
2.	do			
3.	dew			
4.	should			
5.	ooze			
6.	suit			
7.	boutique			
8.	fool			
9.	duke			
10.	two			

Transcription Exercise 12–2

🔊 **AUDIO 2–28**

Vowel: /u/

Refer to Study Card: 35

Phonetic Symbol	Target Word	Transcription
/u/	1. rule	rul
	2. sue	su
	3. loose	lus
	4. rue	
	5. loop	
	6. flew	
	7. sloop	
	8. pool	
	9. fool	

/u/

Distinctive Features	Tongue Position
High, back, tense rounded vowel	Back of tongue is raised high and tense in oral cavity.
	Sides of back of tongue close against upper molars.
	Tongue tip is behind lower front teeth.
	Lips are rounded.

Voicing/Velopharyngeal Port	Spelling Variations
Voiced—vocal folds *add*uct.	Occurs most frequently as "oo" as in b*oo*t, c*oo*l, t*oo*
VP port is closed.	o d*o*, wh*o*
	ew bl*ew*, gr*ew*
	ou s*ou*p, gr*ou*p
	ui fr*ui*t, br*ui*se
	R*oo*f, r*oo*t, h*oo*p can be pronounced with either /u/ or /ʊ/

Word Position	Clinical Information
Medial and final position in SAE	Rarely occurs in Initial position in SAE, such as "*oo*ps."

/ʊ/

Transcription Exercise 12–3   🔊 AUDIO 2–29

		I	M	F
1.	full			
2.	oops			
3.	wolf			
4.	mutt			
5.	soot			
6.	goof			
7.	whoops			
8.	sugar			
9.	footstool			
10.	hood			

Transcription Exercise 12–4

Vowel: /ʊ/

◀)) **AUDIO 2–30**

Refer to Study Card: 36

Phonetic Symbol	Target Word	Transcription
/ʊ/	1. cook	kʊk
	2. wool	wʊl
	3. foot	fʊt
	4. wood	
	5. look	
	6. wolf	
	7. full	
	8. could	
	9. nook	

/ʊ/

Distinctive Features	Tongue Position
High, back-lax, rounded vowel	Sides of back of tongue close lightly against upper molars.
	Sides of back of tongue close lightly against upper molars.
	Back of tongue is raised high in oral cavity.
	Tongue tip touches behind lower front teeth.
	Teeth are slightly open.
	Lips are rounded.
	Airflow is through the oral cavity.

Voicing/Velopharyngeal Port	Spelling Variations
Voiced— vocal folds *ad*duct.	oo b*oo*k, l*oo*k, w*oo*l
VP port is closed.	u p*u*ll
	ou c*ou*ld, w*ou*ld

Word Position	Clinical Information
Medial position only in SAE	Also known as the upsilon or capped "u."

/o/

Transcription Exercise 12–5   🔊)) **AUDIO 2–31**

		I	M	F
1.	old			
2.	moot			
3.	sew			
4.	lotion			
5.	mow			
6.	who			
7.	cola			
8.	toast			
9.	bowl			
10.	macho			

Transcription Exercise 12–6

🔊 **AUDIO 2–32**

Vowel: /o/

Refer to Study Card: 37

Phonetic Symbol	Target Word	Transcription
/o/	1. note	noʊt
	2. tone	toʊn
	3. own	oʊn
	4. tote	
	5. know	
	6. oat	
	7. hone	
	8. no	
	9. owe	

/o/

Distinctive Features	Tongue Position
Midback tense, rounded vowel	Body of tongue shifts slightly back of center and is raised.
	Tongue tip contacts lower front teeth.
	Lips round and protrude.
Voicing/Velopharyngeal Port	**Spelling Variations**
Voiced—vocal folds *ad*duct.	o old, go, no
VP port is closed.	oa coat, boat
	ow crow, know
	oe doe
	ew sew
Word Positions	**Clinical Information**
Initial, medial, and final position in SAE	Some phoneticians refer to this phoneme as the diphthong /oʊ/.

/ɔ/

Transcription Exercise 12–7   🔊)) **AUDIO 2–33**

		I	M	F
1.	all			
2.	thong			
3.	sauce			
4.	awe			
5.	schwa			
6.	moth			
7.	pa			
8.	squaw			
9.	paw			
10.	thought			

Note. Dependent on geographic location, speakers may use /ɑ/ when pronouncing these words.

Transcription Exercise 12–8

Vowel /ɔ/

🔊)) AUDIO 2–34

Refer to Study Card: 38

Phonetic Symbol	Target Word	Transcription
/ɔ/	1. sought	sɔt
	2. bawdy	bɔdi
	3. wrought	rɔt
	4. prawn	
	5. call	
	6. taut	
	7. thought	
	8. vault	
	9. lawful	

Note. Dependent on geographic location, speakers may use /a/ when pronouncing these words.

/ɔ/

Distinctive Features	Tongue Position
Low, midback, lax-rounded vowel	Back and middle portion of tongue is slightly raised.
	Tongue tip touches behind lower front incisors.
	Lips round and protrude slightly.

Voicing/Velopharyngeal Port	Spelling Variations
Voiced—vocal folds *ad*duct.	au *au*to, applause, laundry
VP port is closed.	aw awe, lawn, jaw
	augh(t) caught, taught
	o off, strong
	a ball, call

Word Positions	Clinical Information
Initial, medial, and final position in SAE	Also referred to as the "open o" or "reversed c"
	Edwards (2003) finds this sound very interesting. The /ɔ/ can be affected by a speaker's dialect. The /ɔ/ is not used consistently in Standard American English.

/ɑ/

Transcription Exercise 12–9

		I	M	F
1.	pasta			
2.	almond			
3.	spa			
4.	launch			
5.	genre			
6.	yacht			
7.	aqua			
8.	lunch			
9.	schwa			
10.	entree			

Transcription Exercise 12–10   🔊 **AUDIO 2–36**

Vowel: /ɑ/   Refer to Study Card: 39

Phonetic Symbol	Target Word	Transcription
/ɑ/	1. ah	
	2. not	nɑt
	3. ha	hɑ
	4. yacht	jɑt
	5. tot	
	6. yon	
	7. haunt	
	8. taught	
	9. aunt	

Note. Dependent on geographic location, speakers may use /ɔ/ when pronouncing these words.

/ɑ/

Distinctive Features	Tongue Position
Low, back, lax-unrounded vowel	Tongue is slightly raised in back.
	Tip touches behind lower front teeth.
	Lips do not round or protrude.

Voicing/Velopharyngeal Port	Spelling Variations
Voiced—vocal folds *ad*duct.	o *pot, dot, o*live
VP port is closed.	a *he*a*rt*
	en *en*core

Word Positions	Clinical Information
Initial, medial, and final position in SAE	Used to transcribe the popular expression "ah"

Crossword Puzzle for /u/, /ʊ/, /o/, /ɑ/, and /ɔ/

Answers in Appendix B

1	■	2		
3			4	

Directions: Transcribe the following words:

Across:
3. awful
5. long
6. toe
7. soak

Down:
1. thong
2. foot
4. low
5. loose

BACK VOWELS

Word Search #15   Answers in Appendix B

```
s  ʃ  r  ɑ  dʒ ɚ  d  ɔ  l  t  r  i  z  v  m  f  kʍ
d  ʒ  ɚ  k  j  u  ə  b  ɑ  ɑ  z  ð  ʌ  ɝ  ɑ  n  ɪ
b  ʌ  dʒ ɔ  z  j  o  r  ɑ  r  i  ɛ  v  æ  ʌ  k
ʊ  k  p  s  θ  i  s  ɑ  ɛ  t  æ  ɪ  w  m  n  u  d
l  r  ɛ  k  h  n  dʒ b  ʊ  g  s  z  ð  e  d  o  r
w  ʌ  p  z  s  u  z  ɪ  n  l  u  tʃ i  w  m  ɔ
ɪ  p  v  t  ð  i  z  n  z  ɪ  l  o  p  h  ɑ  d  m
ŋ  æ  k  s  ʃ  u  kʍ h  f  n  v  ɛ  o  b  k  f  ɑ
k  s  g  t  o  θ  p  ʊ  m  p  ʒ  o  p  s  ɛ  ɪ  g
l  ɪ  u  æ  l  j  h  d  ʊ  g  ŋ  m  n  p  t  l  r
b  w  f  e  w  o  k  ʍ  tʃ ɪ  o  u  e  i  l  z  ɔ
h  ɑ  i  ə  ʌ  g  ɑ  r  θ  b  r  ʊ  k  s  o  g  s
n  k  w  tʃ æ  z  ʌ  z  h  t  w  b  v  u  n  ʒ  d
s  kʍ ɪ  k  d  r  ɔ  m  ə  g  r  ɔ  j  h  i  g  t
j  r  u  p  ɔ  l  ɚ  f  ɛ  ɝ  b  f  dʒ u  w  e  l
l  ks ɪ  dʒ o  r  dʒ b  ʊ  ʃ  t  s  f  z  r  s  n
```

Directions: Find and circle the words that contain the /u/ʊ/o/ɑ/ɔ/ phonemes.

The Pope   Jewel
Garth Brooks   RuPaul
Ma and Pa Kettle   Robin Hood
George Bush   Quick Draw McGraw
Jaws   Susan Lucci

Transcription Exercise 12–11

Back Vowels: /u/ʊ/o/ɔ/ɑ/

1. coupon   kupɔn

2. hook   hʊk

3. encore   ankɔr

4. hawthorn   _____

5. newsroom   nuzrum

6. taco   takoʊ

7. yoyo   _____

8. awful   _____

9. yacht   _____

10. lollipop   _____

11. cookbook   _____

12. boastful   _____

13. footstool _____

14. horseshoe _____

15. fought   _____

16. dorm room _____

17. fruit   _____

18. mothball   _____

19. soak   _____

20. thoughtful _____

STUDY QUESTIONS

1. Which back vowel has the greatest mandibular opening?

_____

_____

2. What is the lip position for the majority of back vowels?

_____

_____

3. What is the Greek name for /ʊ/?

_____

_____

4. Which back vowels are produced with rounded lips?

_____

_____

5. List four words that contain the /ʊ/ phoneme.

_____

_____

CHAPTER

13

Diphthongs

Learning Objectives

After reading this chapter, you will be able to:

1. Define diphthongs.

2. Explain how a diphthong is produced.

3. State what is used to indicate how two vowels sounds are used together.

4. Identify which diphthongs are off-glides and on-glides.

5. Transcribe words using diphthongs.

A *diphthong* represents two vowels that are spoken one after the other in continuation, as in saying a single vowel. The first vowel rapidly "glides" into the position of the second vowel. Simply, a diphthong begins by approximating the articulatory position of one vowel and ends by approximating the articulatory position of another vowel. It should be noted that *diphthong* can be pronounced in two ways: [dɪfθaŋ] or [dɪpθaŋ].

Diphthongs are not just the sum total of one vowel plus another, but are a grad-ual movement of the articulators from one position to another. Figure 13–1 illustrates this movement. You will notice that the "capped a" is a component of the /aɪ/ and /aʊ/ diphthongs.

To indicate that the two vowel sounds in each diphthong are used together, a slur ‿ is used. The diphthongs /aɪ/, /aʊ/, and /ɔɪ/ are off-glides, made with the tongue moving from a lower vowel to a high vowel position. The /ju/ is an on-glide, with movement from a higher sound to a lower vowel position.

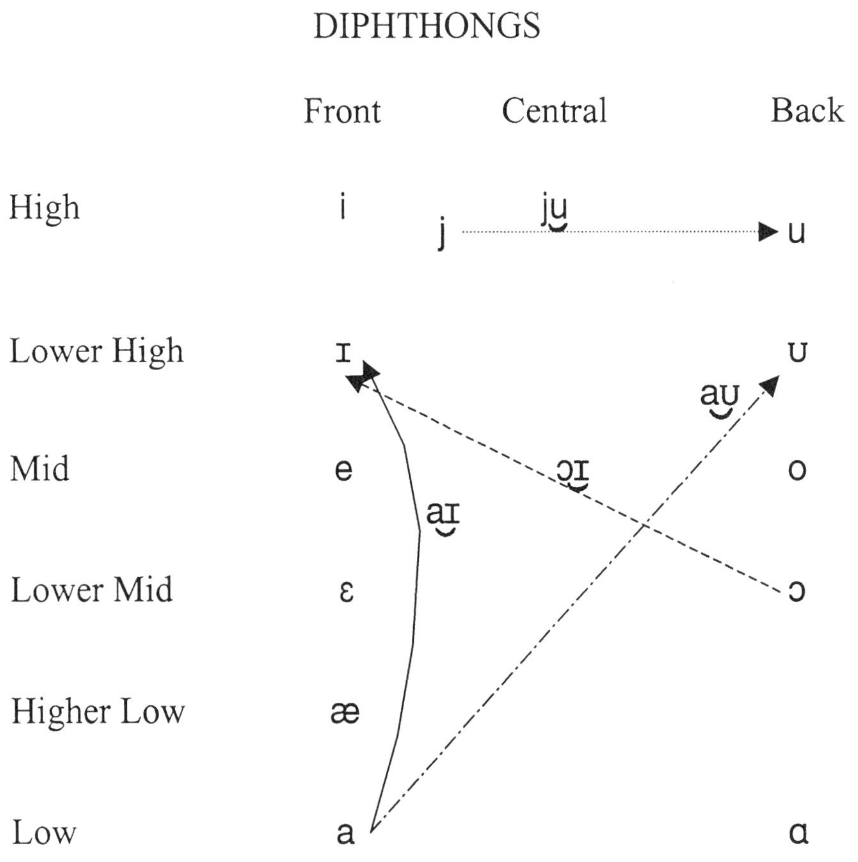

DIPHTHONGS

	Front	Central	Back
High	i	j ·········· ju ·········· →	u
Lower High	ɪ		ʊ aʊ
Mid	e	ɔɪ	o
Lower Mid	ɛ		ɔ
Higher Low	æ		
Low	a		ɑ

aɪ

Figure 13–1. Movement of articulators when producing diphthongs.

/aɪ/

Transcription Exercise 13–1

 **AUDIO 2–38**

		I	M	F
1.	island			
2.	eye			
3.	guy			
4.	minus			
5.	dial			
6.	rhyme			
7.	sweet			
8.	high			
9.	niece			
10.	bride			

Transcription Exercise 13–2

🔊 **AUDIO 2–39**

Diphthong: /aɪ/

Refer to Study Card: 40

Phonetic Symbol	Target Word	Transcription
/aɪ/	1. buy	baɪ
	2. cider	saɪdər
	3. height	haɪt
	4. feisty	
	5. slice	
	6. thyme	
	7. write	
	8. sigh	
	9. rhyme	

/aɪ/

Distinctive Features	Tongue Position
Rising low front to high front (off-glide) diphthong	Tongue is low in the oral cavity.
	Tongue moves from low front position of /a/ to high front position of /ɪ/.

/ɪ/

/a/

Voicing/Velopharyngeal Port	Spelling Variations
Voiced—vocal folds *ad*duct.	i w*i*ld, ch*i*ld, *i*dea
VP port is closed.	ia d*ia*mond
	i-e b*i*ke, *i*ce, k*i*te
	y fr*y*, m*y*, wh*y*
	ie cr*ie*d, p*ie*, l*ie*
	igh he*igh*t, n*igh*

Word Positions	Clinical Information
Initial, medial, and final positions in SAE	Also referred to as the "long i"

/aʊ/

Transcription Exercise 13–3

 AUDIO 2–40

		I	M	F
1.	ouch			
2.	lawn			
3.	coward			
4.	vowel			
5.	how			
6.	toffee			
7.	shout			
8.	know			
9.	lounge			
10.	house			

Transcription Exercise 13–4

Diphthong: /aʊ/

🔊 AUDIO 2–41

Refer to Study Card: 41

Phonetic Symbol	Target Word	Transcription
/aʊ/	1. oust	aʊst
	2. trout	traʊt
	3. gouging	
	4. prowl	
	5. chowder	tʃaʊdɚ
	6. household	
	7. bound	
	8. louse	
	9. bough	

5. tʃaʊdɚ
2. or tʃraʊt

/aʊ/

Distinctive Features	Tongue Position
Rising low front to high back (off-glide) diphthong	Tongue is in low front position for /a/ and glides back to high back position of /ʊ/.

/ʊ/

/a/

Voicing/Velopharyngeal Port	Spelling Variations
Voiced—vocal folds *ad*duct. VP port is closed.	ou *out, house, thou* ow *owl, town, vow*

Word Positions	Clinical Information
Initial, medial, and final positions in SAE	

/ɔɪ/

Transcription Exercise 13–5

 AUDIO 2–42

		I	M	F
1.	coy			
2.	choice			
3.	town			
4.	join			
5.	cipher			
6.	moist			
7.	mist			
8.	buoyant			
9.	juice			
10.	spoil			

Transcription Exercise 13–6

Diphthong: /ɔɪ/

🔊 **AUDIO 2–43**

Refer to Study Card: 42

Phonetic Symbol	Target Word	Transcription
/ɔɪ/	1. hoisting	
	2. coiled	
	3. destroy	
	4. foils	
	5. loiter	
	6. voicing	
	7. toy	tɔɪ
	8. exploit	ɛksplɔɪt
	9. avoid	əvɔɪd

/ɔɪ/

Distinctive Features	Tongue Position
Rising midback to high front (off-glide) diphthong	Tongue glides from lower midback position of /ɔ/ to high front /ɪ/; lips unrounded.

Voicing/Velopharyngeal Port	Spelling Variations
Voiced—vocal folds *ad*duct. VP port is closed.	oi *oil*, c*oi*n oy *oy*ster, l*oy*al, j*oy*

Word Position	Clinical Information
Initial, medial, and final positions in SAE	Also transcribed as /ɔɪ/

/ju/

Transcription Exercise 13–7

 **AUDIO 2–44**

		I	M	F
1.	few			
2.	union			
3.	beauty			
4.	cute			
5.	pew			
6.	use			
7.	huge			
8.	fool			
9.	humor			
10.	hula			

Transcription Exercise 13–8

🔊 **AUDIO 2–45**

Diphthong: /ju/

Refer to Study Card: 43

Phonetic Symbol	Target Word	Transcription
/ju/	1. uke	
	2. fuchsia	
	3. music	
	4. huge	
	5. mutant	
	6. pupil	
	7. spewed	
	8. butte	
	9. fume	

/ju/

Distinctive Features	Tongue Position
High front to high back on-glide diphthong	Tip is at lower front teeth.
	Body of tongue is raised toward hard palate.
	Tongue moves to high back position of /u/.

Voicing/Velopharyngeal Port	Spelling Variations
Voiced—vocal folds *ad*duct.	u *u*nit
VP port is closed.	u-e *use*
	eau *beau*ty
	ew f*ew*

Word Positions	Clinical Information
Initial, medial, and final positions in SAE	

Crossword Puzzle for /a͡ɪ/, /a͡ʊ/, /ɔ͡ɪ/, and /j͡u/

Answers in Appendix B

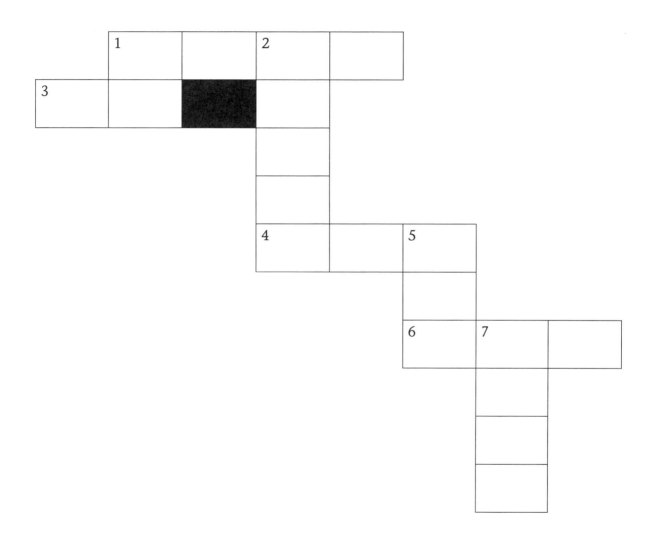

Directions: Transcribe the following words:

Across:

1. moist
3. cue
4. down
6. nine

Down:

1. mew
2. spoiled
5. noun
7. eyesight

DIPHTHONGS

Word Search #16   Answers in Appendix B

```
s   ʃ   r   d   o   n   p   ɚ   r   ɔ   t   t   v
h   aɪ  æ   k   s   v   ju  z   p   n   ə   v   ʌ
d   s   t   ə   ɛ   c   ɛ   b   ɔ   ɔɪ  n   r   d
b   h   i   n   b   w   w   r   b   s   z   f   k
s   aʊ  ɛ   t   k   z   ʌ   u   ʊ   t   i   h   p
h   s   aʊ  θ   b   aʊ  n   d   m   ɚ   b   ju  s
f   p   ʒ   m   ɪ   g   z   i   m   ʒ   u   m   n
k   æ   w   aɪ  l   d   f   aʊ  l   æ   ʊ   ɚ   p
l   ɛ   t   n   æ   k   h   ʌ   ɪ   k   s   n   æ
b   b   s   θ   p   ə   r   z   d   p   i   g   s
h   ɪ   f   ŋ   s   ɔɪ  l   v   z   ɔɪ  v   ʒ   z
n   ju  æ   l   ks  dʒ  t   ʃ   e   z   i   z   f
s   b   z   f   ju  ʃ   ə   t   r   w   g   ɔ   aɪ
o   ɪ   k   aʊ  tʃ  g   j   r   æ   m   ɑ   ɚ   j
```

Directions: Find and circle the words listed below that contain the /aɪ/aʊ/ɔɪ/ju/ phonemes.

icehouse	wildfowl	soil
fuchsia	high	mine
poise	humor	oyster
you	views	couch
southbound		

Transcription Exercise 13–9

Diphthongs: /aɪ/aʊ/ɔɪ/ju/

🔊)) **AUDIO 2–46**

Phoneme Study Cards: 40–43

1. foundry   faʊndri or faʊndʒri

2. join   dʒɔɪn

3. Yukon

4. brine   braɪn

5. toil

6. January

7. oust   aʊst

8. ukulele

9. moist

10. amulet

11. pout

12. byte

13. noun

14. noise

15. frowning

16. I

17. contributor

18. oink

19. mime

20. brownies

STUDY QUESTIONS

1. What does a diphthong represent?

   _____

   _____

2. Why are diphthongs not considered a combination of vowels?

   _____

   _____

3. How is a slur written?

   _____

   _____

4. What diphthongs are off-glides?

   _____

   _____

5. What is the on-glide diphthong?

   _____

   _____

6. What diphthong is referred to as "long i"?

   _____

   _____

CHAPTER

14

Word Stress

Learning Objectives

After reading this chapter, you will be able to:

1. Define stress as it relates to syllables.

2. Identify three features associated with stress.

3. Describe how stress can change a noun to a verb.

4. State four ways to determine syllable stress.

5. Explain the use of stress and morphological markers.

6. Identify primary stress in two to four syllable words.

This chapter reviews the basics of stress. The term *stress* is often used interchangeably with the term *accent*. Stress refers to the most prominent part of a syllable in a multisyllabic word, or word within a phrase. Greater breath force creates this emphasis. Singh and Singh (2006) states stress has been associated with (a) high amplitude (loudness), (b) long duration of the syllable nucleus (time), and (c) high frequency (pitch) of the syllable nucleus. Singh concludes that stressing syllables or words requires increased effort on the part of the speaker. He also adds that the result is that some words or parts of words stand out more than others, making it easier for the listener to grasp the most important meaningful elements of the message.

In words of more than one syllable, one syllable will usually receive more stress than the other. For example, the first syllable of "hap-py" receives more stress than the second syllable. In addition, stress can serve a *phonemic* function. A change in stressed syllable changes word meaning. For example, the first syllable of the noun "'rebel" receives primary (or greatest) stress. However, if the second syllable is stressed, it is changed into the verb re'bel.

Determining stress is not always easy. Garn-Nunn and Lynn (2004) view assignment of stress in English as very erratic due to the speaker following conventional usage. American English speakers are familiar with word pronunciation. This is an area where English second-language learners can have difficulty. One *very simple* way in which to determine syllable stress is to place stress on the *wrong* syllable. If you heard someone say "IMportant" rather than "imPORtant" it would sound unusual to you. Figure 14–1 provides an example of how stress in a word can produce a laugh. Here are some helpful hints to determine stress:

1 One-syllable words spoken in isolation always receive primary stress.

2 The majority of two-syllable words have stress on the first syllable.

3 Compound verbs have primary stress on the second verb, such as in "over*throw.*"

4 Compound words of two syllables have the same amount of stress on each word (cupcake).

The International Phonetic Association alphabet suggests using three distinct stress levels in English multisyllabic words, described as: (a) *primary stress* with the stress mark ['] in front of the syllable receiving primary stress, (b) *secondary stress* [ˌ], (c) and no symbol to indicate *unstress*. However, the "stress" of this chapter focuses on assigning primary stress on the first or second syllable, as this can be most helpful. The reader is

"African Elephant"
(Af-rican)

Figure 14–1. An example of how changing the stress of a word can make an amusing difference: *From the journal of a preschool teacher:* "All of my five-year-old students are learning to read. Yesterday, one student pointed to a picture in a zoo book and said, 'Look! It's a frickin' elephant!' I took a deep breath, then asked, 'What did you call it?' The child responded, 'It's a frickin' elephant! It says so on the picture!' And so it did . . ."

referred to Edwards (2003) and Singh and Singh (2006) for further discussion of secondary stress.

Adding a prefix or suffix usually does not cause a change in primary stress. Table 14–1 provides examples of morphological markers.

Table 14–1. Syllable Stress and Examples of Morphological Markers

| Morphological Marker | Base Word | Number of Syllables | Primary Syllable Stress | | Transcription |
			1st	2nd	
Regular plural -s	plants	1	X		[plænts]
Regular plural -z	signs	1	X		[saɪnz]
Regular plural -ez	bunches	2	X		[bʌntʃɛz]
3rd Person					
Regular present tense -s	sits	1	X		[sɪts]
Regular present tense -z	runs	1	X		[rʌnz]
Regular present tense -ez	crashes	2	X		[kræʃɛz]
Regular past tense -t	walked	1	X		[wɑkt]
Regular past tense -d	plugged	1	X		[plʌgd]
Regular past tense -ed	waited	2	X		[wetɪd]
Present progressive -ing	walking	2	X		[wɔlkɪŋ]

Important Note: As you can see, prefixes and suffixes (including possessives and modifiers) do not have primary stress on the second syllable.

Exercise 14–1

 **AUDIO 2–47**

This exercise provides practice in identifying primary stress in two syllable words. Listen carefully to hear which syllable is stressed. Stressed syllable is in **bold** print.

First Syllable Primary Stress	Second Syllable Primary Stress
1. **teach**er	1. de**ter**
2. **prior**	2. a**bove**
3. **mor**al	3. o**bey**
4. **sadd**le	4. sham**poo**
5. **hap**py	5. a**mass**
6. **ta**co	6. in**fect**
7. **fad**ed	7. be**side**
8. **in**jure	8. re**main**
9. **care**ful	9. a**fraid**
10. **fun**ny	10. as**sist**

Transcription Exercise 14–2    AUDIO 2–48

Listen to these words in which primary stress changes the meaning of the word. The first five have been completed for you. See Appendix B for answers.

1. 'digest   1. di' gest

2. 'contest   2. con' test

3. 'rebel   3. re' bel

4. 'produce   4. pro' duce

5. 'address   5. ad' dress

6. _____   6. _____

7. _____   7. _____

8. _____   8. _____

9. _____   9. _____

10. _____   10. _____

Transcription Exercise 14–3

 AUDIO 2–49

After listening to these words pronounced on the audio file, decide which syllable has primary stress in these two, three, and four-syllable words. Remember to place the primary stress mark before the syllable that has primary stress. Answers in Appendix B.

	Syllable Division	# of Syllables
1. licorice		
2. ingredient		
3. crying		
4. another		
5. audible		
6. hilarious		
7. security		
8. computer		
9. saxophone		
10. bigger		
11. pleasure		
12. aggravation		
13. aftermath		
14. resource		
15. prepare		
16. liberal		
17. watermelon		
18. generation		
19. evaporate		
20. public		

STUDY QUESTIONS

1. What is another term for stress?

_____

_____

2. Define stress.

_____

_____

3. How does stress function to change a noun to a verb?

_____

_____

4. How do morphological markers affect word stress?

_____

_____

5. How are components of compound words of two syllables stressed?

_____

_____

6. According to Singh and Singh (2006), name three features of stress.

_____

_____

15

Dynamics of Connected Speech

Learning Objectives

After reading this chapter, you will be able to:

1. Define an accommodation and state two types.

2. State the difference between progressive and regressive assimilation.

3. Describe the process of intrusion of /t/ in the word "mince."

4. Define diacritic and give examples in words.

5. Explain coarticulation.

6. Define phonetic environment/context.

Introduction

By the time you read this chapter, you have spent numerous hours studying the IPA to memorize the phonetic symbols and completing the Transcription Exercises. In this chapter, you learn about the interesting changes in words that can occur during speech. The renowned linguist, Peter Ladefoged, compares the rapid tongue move-ments required for speech to that of a concert pianist's rapid finger movements (2005, p. 185). During speech, considerable effort is expended by muscles of the tongue, jaw, lips, velum, and laryngeal region to produce the finely timed precision movements required to distinctly articulate each phoneme. According to Shipley and McAfee (2008), conversational speech is uttered at the incredible speed of 270 words per minute.

To cope with this task of articulating extremely rapid changes from phoneme to phoneme, *accommodation* occurs. Accommodation is an adjustment or adaptation of a speech sound as a result of the *phonetic environment* (or *context*) of a phoneme. Phonetic environment describes the phonemes that surround a specific speech sound. There are two types of accommodation, *assimilation* and *coarticulation.*

Assimilation produces major changes that occur when a phoneme is omitted, added, or changed to a different phoneme.

Coarticulation produces minor changes in phonemes. Phoneticians disagree on whether the processes of coarticulation and assimilation are two distinct processes, or are similar. We support MacKay (1987) in his view of two processes.

Assimilation

There are two types of assimilation: *progressive* and *regressive assimilation.* These types of assimilation can result in a change in place of production and/or voicing of a phoneme.

Progressive Assimilation

Say the word "dogs." When articulated, the word is transcribed as [dɑgz]. Progressive assimilation has occurred in this word in a left-to-right pattern. The voicing of the /g/ has influenced the unvoiced /s/, changing it into the voiced /z/. The *preceding* phoneme /g/ has influenced the phoneme that follows, /s/. Progressive assimilation occurs as a function of *morphology,* or the study of *morphemes.* According to McLaughlin (2006), a *morpheme* is a minimal, meaningful unit of language. Of the two types of morphemes, free and bound, we focus on the *bound* morphemes, which must be attached to a word.

Some examples of these are the –s as in coughs [kɑfs], -z as in runs [rʌnz], and the regular past tense –d as in mobbed [mɑbd]. See Table 15–1 for examples of bound morphemes in nouns and regular past-tense verbs. As discussed previously, progressive assimilation occurs as a function of morphology. Here are some examples of bound morphemes in nouns and regular past-tense verbs. Transcription Exercise 15–1 will give you practice for this concept.

Regressive Assimilation

In contrast to progressive assimilation, the effects of regressive assimilation occur in a right-to-left manner. In this type of assimilation, a phoneme is changed by the phoneme that *follows* it. For example, in the word "bank," the /k/ influences the preceding /n/ phoneme by changing it into an /ŋ/. The correct transcription would be [beŋk].

Unless each phoneme is produced with a pause before and after, as in "b-a-n-k" (which would sound unusual), the effects of regressive assimilation cannot be avoided. The reason this occurs is that the place of articulation of the /k/ (lingua-velar) affects the place of articulation of the /n/ (lingua-alveolar), and the /n/ *assimilates* the place of articulation of the /ŋ/, which is also a lingua-velar.

Another example of regressive assimilation occurs in the word "horseshoe." The final sound of /s/ in "horse" is completely assimilated into the prolonged initial sound of "shoe" /ʃ/, so the word is transcribed as [horʃu].

Transcription Exercise 15–1 contains opportunities for transcription of words with regressive assimilation.

Phonemes can also be omitted during speech. The word "veteran" [vɛtə˞ɪn] is often pronounced [vɛtrɪn]. Omission, also called *elision,* occurs very frequently in phrases.

Table 15–1. Bound Morpheme Examples

Plural nouns.

Note. If the final consonant of a word is voiced, the bound morpheme will be a voiced phoneme. Remember, because all vowels are voiced, the bound morpheme will be voiced as in jaws [dʒɔz].

Nouns - plural -z		Nouns - plural -s	
beds	[bɛdz]	baskets	[bæskɛts]
airplane	[ɛrplenz]	snaps	[snæps]
bells	[bɛlz]	faiths	[feθs]
doors	[dorz]	chefs	[ʃɛfs]
clowns	[klaʊnz]	desks	[dɛsks]
birds	[bɝdz]	biceps	[baɪsɛps]
rugs	[rʌgz]	rocks	[rɑks]
pans	[pænz]	ships	[ʃɪps]
tubs	[tʌbz]	boots	[buts]
kings	[kɪŋz]	clerks	[klɝks]

Regular past tense verbs.

Note. -ed in a word is produced as /t/ when following an unvoiced phoneme, and -ed in a word is produced as /d/ when following a voiced phoneme.

Verbs past tense -t		Verbs past tense -d	
wished	[wɪʃt]	pinned	[pɪnd]
punched	[pʌntʃt]	sagged	[sægd]
kicked	[kɪkt]	hummed	[hʌmd]
chased	[tʃest]	waved	[wevd]
looked	[lʊkt]	drained	[drend]
raced	[rest]	smoothed	[smuðd]
mixed	[mɪkst]	fanned	[fænd]
laughed	[læft]	signed	[saɪnd]
snapped	[snæpt]	wedged	[wɛdʒd]
smirked	[smɝkt]	wagged	[wægd]

The phrase, "Where have you been?" can be shortened to [wɛrjʌbɪn].

In contrast to phoneme elimination, some sounds can be added, a process known as *epenthesis* or *intrusion*. The /t/ phoneme is a common intrusive sound, especially when a nasal sound is followed by an unvoiced sound. Say the word "mince." An interesting thing occurs when the word "mince" is articulated. Unless we pause between saying the /n/ and /s/ sounds (which would sound unusual), the word is articulated as [mɪnᵗs]. You will notice the addition of the /t/ that has been intruded. In producing the word "mince," the tongue is at the alveolar ridge for the /n/, which is also where the /s/ is produced. To make articulation easier, the tongue *remains* at the alveolar ridge, with the result of the intruded /t/. The /n,s,t/ are all produced in the same *place* of articulation. Intrusion is defined as the addition of a sound that is not included in the spelling of the word, but which occurs when the word is articulated.

Remember that the intruded sound may or not be audible, but is present because it is articulated. Some phoneticians choose to raise the intruded /t/ when a word is transcribed. Intrusion is a result of the speed with which we speak and the economical articulatory movements.

The /p/ and /k/ phonemes are also subject to intrusion. The word "warmth" is transcribed as [wormpθ], with the intrusion of the /p/. In order to eliminate the intruded /p/, the speaker would have to pause between saying the /m/ and the /θ/. An example of the intruded /k/ occurs in the word "length," which is articulated as [leŋkθ]. Try saying each phoneme separately in the word "length," and then say the word as you normally would by blending the sounds together.

Unlike the /t/p/k/, which intrude in the phonetic context of other consonants, the /j/ and /w/ can intrude between vowels. In the phrase "see it," the /j/ intrudes between the final position vowel of the first word /i/ and the initial vowel /ɪ/ of the word which follows, as in [sijɪt]. The phrase "two apples" provides an example of the intruded /w/, as in [tuwæpəlz]. If the words in the phrases were said separately, the intrusion of /j/ and /w/ would not occur.

Coarticulation

The other type of accommodation is coarticulation. Compared to the major changes in assimilation, coarticulation produces *minor* phonetic changes. Coarticulation occurs as a result of a fast rate of speech. Say the word "moon." Did you notice that your lips were already in position for the /u/ when you were producing the /m/? In Standard American English, vowels are normally produced without nasal resonance, except when they appear before or after a nasal consonant, as in [mæ̃n]. This nasality is indicated by the /~/ symbol placed over the sound that has acquired nasal resonance. Symbols that indicate a specific way a phoneme has been produced are termed *diacritics*. This is *narrow transcription,* which uses diacritics to specifically explain how a sound was produced. Contrast this with *broad transcription*, which uses only the IPA phoneme symbol to represent a sound.

Frequently used diacritics are listed in Table 15–2. S. Singh and K. Singh (2006) provide an expanded list of diacritics.

Often in conversational speech, we extend the duration of a sound, known as *lengthening* or *prolongation*. This occurs frequently when we say two words together, one of which ends in the same sound as the beginning sound of the adjacent word. For example, the phrase "same milk" can be produced as [semːɪlk]. The lengthening diacritic [ː] *follows* the prolonged phoneme.

We can say the phrase "both thumbs" as two separate words, or joined together as in [boθːʌmz]. The diacritic [ː] is used to indicate lengthening. Some examples are provided in Transcription Exercise 15–1.

Another change that can occur in speech is *devoicing*. Devoicing occurs when a voiced phoneme becomes unvoiced due to the phonetic environment, but the voiced phoneme does *not* become totally voiceless. The phonetic environment for devoicing is when

Table 15–2. Selected Diacritics

Diacritic	Name	Example	Affects	Phoneme(s)
[ʰ]	Aspirated	[pʰost]	Voiceless stops	/p/, /t /, /k/
[˺]	Unreleased	[bæk˺drɔp]	All plosives	/p/, /b/, /t /, /d/, /k/, /g/
[˜]	Nasality	[nõt]	Vowels adjacent to nasals	All vowels & diphthongs
[̥]	Unvoiced	[pr̥ɑɪ]	Follows voiceless consonants	/r/
[̬]	Voiced	[bɛt̬ɚ]	Adjacent to voiced sounds	/t/, /s/
[̩]	Syllabic consonant	[bʌtn̩] [æpl̩]	Lateral and nasals	/l/, /n/, /m/, /ŋ/
[ː]	Prolongation	[dɑːrk]	Emphasized phonemes	Possible with any phonemes

a voiced phoneme follows an unvoiced phoneme, as in the word "pray" [pr̥e]. The devoicing diacritic is a small circle / ̥/ *under* the devoiced phoneme.

Here is a silly sentence that uses the diacritics discussed in this chapter:

Put these zany dogs in the backdoor of the clean critter kennel.

[pʊtʰ ðizːeñi dɑgz ɪn ði bæk˺ dor ʌv ði kl̥in kr̥ɪt̬ɚ kɛnl̩]

Transcription Exercise 15–1

 **AUDIO 2–50**

These words contain examples of: (1) progressive assimilation, (2) regressive assimilation, (3) intrusion, (4) lengthening, and (5) omission.

1. fixed (1) _____

2. cancel (3) _____

3. stop pushing (4)_____

4. junk (2) _____

5. pushed (1) _____

6. dreamt (3) _____

7. go away (5) _____

8. wigs (1) _____

9. mink (2) _____

10. little Lucy (4) _____

11. fragrance (3) _____

12. stomachs (1) _____

13. kiss her (5) _____

14. comfort (3) _____

15. black corn (4) _____

16. bugs (1) _____

17. let me go (5) _____

18. prince (3) _____

19. seeds (1) _____

20. thin knife (4) _____

STUDY QUESTIONS

1. Define accommodation.

_____

_____

2. Define phonetic context.

_____

_____

3. Name two types of accommodation.

_____

_____

4. What is the difference between progressive and regressive assimilation?

_____

_____

5. Why does coarticulation occur?

_____

_____

6. What is a diacritic?

_____

_____

7. What diacritic represents lengthening?

_____

_____

8. What is a phonetic context for devoicing a voiced phoneme?

_____

_____

9. How do epenthesis and elision differ?

_____

_____

16

Dialect Differences

Learning Objectives

After reading this chapter, you will be able to:

1. Define dialect and accent.

2. Name the major geographic dialect regions in the United States.

3. List articulation characteristics of African American English, Arabic, Spanish, and Asian speakers.

The focus of this Workbook is phoneme production in Standard American English (SAE). SAE is "accent-free." This is the type of speech you hear when you listen to national broadcasters present the news on television and radio. A *dialect* is a speech or language variation. We refer to an *accent* when we discuss speech that has characteristics of a foreign dialect.

There are several United States dialects representative of various geographic regions including the East, Midwest, and Southern states. Each region has specific variations in pronunciation and language.

Speakers of African American English use specific speech substitutions. These are presented in Table 16–1. Foreign accents in the Arabic, Hispanic, and Asian dialects are included in Tables 16–2, 16–3, and 16–4, respectively.

Dolores Battle (Ed.) (2012) offers a detailed discussion of phonological and grammatical differences in numerous languages.

Table 16–1. Characteristics of African American English Articulation and Phonology

Articulation Characteristics	Sample English Utterances
/l/ phoneme lessened or omitted	too'/tool a'ways/always
/r/ phoneme lessened or omitted	doah/door mudah/mother p'otect/protect
f/voiceless "th" substitution at the end or middle of a word	teef/teeth bof/both nuffin'/nothing
t/voiceless "th" substitution at the beginning of a word	tink/think tin/thin
d/voiced "th" substitution at the beginning or middle words	dis/this broder/brother
v/voiced "th" substitution at the end of words	breave/breathe smoov/smooth
Consonant cluster reduction	des'/desk res'/rest lef'/left was'/wasp
Differing syllable stress patterns	**gui** tar/guitar **po** lice/police **Ju** ly/July
Final consonant in verb may change when past tense ending is added	li-tid/liked wah-tid/walked
Metathesis occurs	aks "axe"/ask
Devoicing of final voiced consonants	bet/bed ruk/rug cap/cab
Final consonants may be deleted	ba'/bad goo'/good
High front vowel substituted for midfront vowel "i" replaces "e"	pin/pen tin/ten

Table 16–1. *continued*

Articulation Characteristics	Sample English Utterances
b/v substitution	balentine/valentine
	bes'/best
Diphthong reduction	fahnd/find
	ol/oil
	pond/pound
n/ng substitution	walkin'/walking
	thin'/thing

Source: From *Multicultural Students with Special Language Needs: Practical Strategies for Assessment and Intervention* (4th ed.). (Table 4–2, pp. 79–80), by C. Roseberry-McKibbin, 2014, Oceanside, CA: Academic Communication Associates. Copyright 2014 by Academic Communication Associates. Reprinted with permission.

Table 16–2. Articulation and Language Differences Commonly Observed Among Arabic Speakers

Articulation Characteristics	Possible English Errors	
n/ng substitution	son/song	nothin'/nothing
sh/ch substitution	mush/much	shoe/chew
w/v substitution or f/v substitution	west/vest fife/five	Walerie/Valerie abofe/above
t/voiceless "th" substitution or s/voiceless "th" substitution	bat/bath sing/thing	noting/nothing somesing/something
z/voiced "th" substitution	brozer/brother	zese/these
zh/j substitution	zhoke/joke	fuzh/fudge
retroflex /r/ does not exist	Speakers of Arabic will use a tap or trilled /r/.	
There are no triple consonant clusters in Arabic, so epenthesis may occur	kinduhly/kindly	harduhly/hardly
o/a substitutions	hole/hall	bowl/ball
o/oi substitutions	bowl/boil	foble/foible
uh/a substitutions	snuck/snack	ruck/rack
ee/i substitutions	cheep/chip	sheep/ship
Language Characteristics	**Possible English Errors**	
Omission of possessive 's and "of"	That Kathy book. The title story is . . .	
Omission of plurals	She has 5 horse in her stable. He has 3 pen in his pocket.	
Omissions of prepositions	Put your shoes.	
Omission of the form "to be"	She _____ my friend.	
Inversion of noun constructs	Let's go to the station gas.	

Source: From *Multicultural Students with Special Language Needs: Practical Strategies for Assessment and Intervention* (4th ed.). (Table 9–2, p. 207), by C. Roseberry-McKibbin, 2014, Oceanside, CA: Academic Communication Associates. Copyright 2014 by Academic Communication Associates. Reprinted with permission.

Table 16–3. Articulation Differences Commonly Observed Among Spanish Speakers

Articulation Characteristics	Sample English Patterns	
1. /t, d, n/ may be dentalized (tip of tongue is placed against the back of the upper central incisors).		
2. Final consonants are often devoiced.	dose/doze	
3. b/v substitution	berry/very	
4. Deaspirated stops (sounds like the speaker is omitting the sound because it is said with little air released).		
5. ch/sh substitution	chew/shoe	
6. d/voiced th or z/voiced th (voiced "th" does not exist as a distinct phoneme in Spanish).	dis/this zat/that	
7. t/voiceless th (voiceless "th" does not exist as a distinct phoneme in Spanish).	tink/think	
8. Schwa sound is inserted before word initial consonant clusters.	eskate/skate espend/spend	
9. In Spanish, words can end in 10 different sounds: a, ε, i, o, u, l, r, n, s, d	may omit other sounds at the ends of words	
10. When words start with an "h," the "h" is silent.	'old/hold	'it/hit
11. /r / is tapped or trilled (tap /r / might sound like the tap in the English word "butter")		
12. There is no "j" (e.g., judge) sound in Spanish; speakers may substitute "y."	Yulie/Julie yoke/joke	
13. Spanish /s/ is produced more frontally than English /s/.	Some speakers may sound like they have frontal lisps.	
14. The ñ is produced as "ny" (e.g., baño is pronounced "bahnyo").		
Spanish has 5 vowels: a, e, i, o, u (ah, eh, ee, long o, oo) and few diphthongs. Thus, Spanish speakers may produce the following vowel substitutions:		
15. ee/ih substitution	peeg/pig	leetle/little
16. eh/æ, ah/æ	pet/pat	Stahn, Stan

Source: From *Multicultural Students with Special Language Needs: Practical Strategies for Assessment and Intervention* (4th ed.). (Table 5–2, p. 108), by C. Roseberry-McKibbin, 2014, Oceanside, CA: Academic Communication Associates. Copyright 2014 by Academic Communication Associates. Reprinted with permission.

Table 16–4. Articulation Differences Commonly Observed Among Asian Speakers

Articulation Characteristics	Sample English Utterances	
In many Asian languages, words end in vowels only, or in just a few consonants; speakers may delete many final consonants in English.	ste/step	li/lid
	ro/robe	do/dog
Some languages are monosyllabic; speakers may truncate polysyllabic words or emphasize the wrong syllable.	efunt/elephant	
	diversity/diversity (emphasis on the first syllable)	
Possible devoicing of voiced cognates	beece/bees	pick/pig
	luff/love	crip/crib
r/l confusion	lize/rise	clown/crown
/r/ may be omitted entirely.	gull/girl	tone/torn
Reduction of vowel length in words	Words sound choppy to Americans.	
No voiced or voiceless "th"	dose/those	tin/thin
	zose/those	sin/thin
Epenthesis (addition of "uh" sound in blends, ends of words)	bulack/black	wooduh/wood
Confusion of "ch" and "sh"	sheep/cheap	beesh/beach
/æ/ does not exist in many Asian languages	block/black	shock/shack
b/v substitutions	base/vase	Beberly/Beverly
v/w substitutions	vork/work	vall/wall

STUDY QUESTIONS

1. Standard American English is also identified as:

_____

_____

2. Define dialect.

_____

_____

3. Define accent.

_____

_____

4. Name three dialect regions of the United States.

_____

_____

5. According to Roseberry-McKibbin (2014), name three articulation characteristics of African American English.

_____

_____

6. According to Roseberry-McKibbin (2014), list three articulation characteristics of Spanish speakers.

_____

_____

APPENDIX

The International Phonetic Alphabet

THE INTERNATIONAL PHONETIC ALPHABET (revised to 2015)

© 2015 IPA

CONSONANTS (PULMONIC)

	Bilabial	Labiodental	Dental	Alveolar	Postalveolar	Retroflex	Palatal	Velar	Uvular	Pharyngeal	Glottal
Plosive	p b			t d		ʈ ɖ	c ɟ	k ɡ	q ɢ		ʔ
Nasal	m	ɱ		n		ɳ	ɲ	ŋ	ɴ		
Trill	ʙ			r					ʀ		
Tap or Flap		ⱱ		ɾ		ɽ					
Fricative	ɸ β	f v	θ ð	s z	ʃ ʒ	ʂ ʐ	ç ʝ	x ɣ	χ ʁ	ħ ʕ	h ɦ
Lateral fricative				ɬ ɮ							
Approximant		ʋ		ɹ		ɻ	j	ɰ			
Lateral approximant				l		ɭ	ʎ	ʟ			

Symbols to the right in a cell are voiced, to the left are voiceless. Shaded areas denote articulations judged impossible.

CONSONANTS (NON-PULMONIC)

Clicks	Voiced implosives	Ejectives
ʘ Bilabial	ɓ Bilabial	' Examples:
ǀ Dental	ɗ Dental/alveolar	p' Bilabial
ǃ (Post)alveolar	ʄ Palatal	t' Dental/alveolar
ǂ Palatoalveolar	ɠ Velar	k' Velar
ǁ Alveolar lateral	ʛ Uvular	s' Alveolar fricative

VOWELS

Where symbols appear in pairs, the one to the right represents a rounded vowel.

OTHER SYMBOLS

ʍ	Voiceless labial-velar fricative		ɕ ʑ	Alveolo-palatal fricatives
w	Voiced labial-velar approximant		ɺ	Voiced alveolar lateral flap
ɥ	Voiced labial-palatal approximant		ɧ	Simultaneous ʃ and x
ʜ	Voiceless epiglottal fricative			Affricates and double articulations
ʢ	Voiced epiglottal fricative			can be represented by two symbols
ʡ	Epiglottal plosive			joined by a tie bar if necessary.

$$\widehat{ts} \quad \widehat{kp}$$

SUPRASEGMENTALS

ˈ	Primary stress	ˌfoʊnəˈtɪʃən
ˌ	Secondary stress	
ː	Long	eː
ˑ	Half-long	eˑ
̆	Extra-short	ĕ
|	Minor (foot) group	
‖	Major (intonation) group	
.	Syllable break	ɹi.ækt
‿	Linking (absence of a break)	

TONES AND WORD ACCENTS

LEVEL				CONTOUR		
e̋	or ˥	Extra high	ě	or ↗	Rising
é	˦	High	ê	↘	Falling
ē	˧	Mid	e᷄	↗	High rising
è	˨	Low	e᷅	↗	Low rising
ȅ	˩	Extra low	e᷈	↗	Rising-falling
ꜜ	Downstep		↗	Global rise
ꜛ	Upstep		↘	Global fall

DIACRITICS Some diacritics may be placed above a symbol with a descender, e.g. ŋ̊

̥	Voiceless	n̥ d̥	̤	Breathy voiced	b̤ a̤	̪	Dental	t̪ d̪
̬	Voiced	s̬ t̬	̰	Creaky voiced	b̰ a̰	̺	Apical	t̺ d̺
ʰ	Aspirated	tʰ dʰ	̼	Linguolabial	t̼ d̼	̻	Laminal	t̻ d̻
̹	More rounded	ɔ̹	ʷ	Labialized	tʷ dʷ	̃	Nasalized	ẽ
̜	Less rounded	ɔ̜	ʲ	Palatalized	tʲ dʲ	ⁿ	Nasal release	dⁿ
̟	Advanced	u̟	ˠ	Velarized	tˠ dˠ	ˡ	Lateral release	dˡ
̠	Retracted	e̠	ˤ	Pharyngealized	tˤ dˤ	̚	No audible release	d̚
̈	Centralized	ë	̴	Velarized or pharyngealized	ɫ			
̽	Mid-centralized	e̽	̝	Raised	e̝ (ɹ̝ = voiced alveolar fricative)			
̩	Syllabic	n̩	̞	Lowered	e̞ (β̞ = voiced bilabial approximant)			
̯	Non-syllabic	e̯	̘	Advanced Tongue Root	e̘			
˞	Rhoticity	ɚ a˞	̙	Retracted Tongue Root	e̙			

Answers to Exercises

Chapter 2

Transcription Exercise 2–1
AUDIO 1–2

Number of Sounds			Transcription
2	1.	gnaw	[nɔ]
3	2.	shape	[ʃep]
5	3.	cousin	[kʌzɪn]
4	4.	leisure	[liʒɚ]
3	5.	tongue	[tʌŋ]
2	6.	who	[hu]
4	7.	rather	[ræðɚ]
3	8.	tough	[tʌf]
3	9.	kneel	[nil]
3	10.	ax	[æks]
7	11.	cinnamon	[sɪnʌmɪn]
3	12.	wrap	[ræp]
4	13.	raked	[rekt]
3	14.	sight	[saɪt]
5	15.	phoneme	[fonim]

Transcription Exercise 2–2
AUDIO 1–3

[præktɪs ɛvɚi de]

Transcription Exercise 2–3
AUDIO 1–4

Consonants		Vowels	
1.	/k/	7.	/u/
2.	/ŋ/	8.	/i/
3.	/dʒ/	9.	/o/
4.	/f/	10.	/ɚ/
5.	/j/	11.	/e/
6.	/z/	12.	/ɑ/

Exercise 2–A

Syllable Division	# Syllables
1. co-da	2
2. nu-cle-us	3
3. vow-el	2
4. syl-la-ble	3
5. rhyme	1
6. i-ni-tial	3
7. me-di-al	3
8. fi-nal	2
9. blend	1
10. clus-ter	2
11. ar-rest-ing	3
12. re-leas-ing	3
13. con-so-nant	3
14. or-thog-ra-phy	4
15. pound	1
16. wig-gle	2
17. in-tel-li-gence	4
18. math-e-mat-i-cal	5
19. cen-ti-me-ter	4
20. choc-o-late	3

Exercise 2–B. Syllable Shapes

1. V C   ash
   æ ʃ

2. C C V C   crash
   k r æ ʃ

3. C C C V C   splash
   s p l æ ʃ

4. V C C V C   eastern
   i s t ɚ n

5. C C V C   green
   g r i n

6. C C V   three
   θ r i

7. C C V C   preach
   p r i tʃ

8. C C C V C   scream
   s k r i m

9. C C V C   frame
   f r e m

10. C V C C V C V C   phosphorus
    f ɑ s f o r ə s

Exercise 2–C

1. Brachyceratops
   C C V C V C V C V C V C C
   b r a k i s ɛ r ɑ t ɑ p s

2. Corythosaurus
   C V C V C V C V C V C
   k o r i θ o s ɑ r ə s

3. Dilophosaurus
   C V C V C V C V C V C
   d ɪ l o f o s ɑ r ə s

4. Microceratops
   C V C C V C V C V C V C C
   m aɪ k r o s ɛ r ɑ t ɑ p s

5. Pachyrhinosaurus

C V C V C V C V C V C V C
p æ k i r a͡ɪ n o s a r ə s

6. Pentaceratops

C V C C V C V C V C V C C
p ɛ n t ə s ɛ r a t a p s

7. Triceratops

C C V C V C V C V C C
t r a͡ɪ s ɛ r a t a p s

8. Brachiosaurus

C C V C V V C V C V C
b r a k i o s a r ə s

9. Epachthosaurus

V C V C C V C V C V C
ɛ p æ k θ o s a r ə s

10. Heterodontosaurus

C V C V V C V C C V C V C V C
h ɛ t ɚ o d a n t o s a r ə s

Chapter 3

Exercises 3–A through 3–E

Answers are in **bold** print.

Exercise 3–A. Manner of articulation: Stop-Consonants

1. **B**lack**b**ir**d**
2. **D**ay **T**ripper
3. **G**et **B**ack
4. **P**aper**b**ack Writer
5. **T**icket to Ride
6. A Hard **D**ay's Nigh**t**
7. I **G**ot to Find My **B**aby
8. I'll **B**e **B**ack
9. Come and **G**et I**t**
10. Let It **B**e

Exercise 3–B. Manner of articulation: Nasals

1. If I **N**eeded So**m**eo**n**e
2. Lady **M**ado**nn**a
3. Le**n**d **M**e Your Co**m**b
4. **M**aggie **M**ae
5. Pe**nn**y La**n**e
6. Su**n** Ki**ng**
7. Tax**m**a**n**
8. I'**m** O**n**ly Sleepi**ng**
9. Tip of **M**y To**ng**ue
10. **M**ail**m**a**n**, Bri**ng** **M**e **N**o **M**ore Blues

Exercise 3–C. Manner of articulation: Fricatives

1. Another Girl
2. Strawberry Fields Forever
3. Dizzy Miss Lizzy
4. Good Day Sunshine
5. Here Comes the Sun
6. I Saw Her Standing There
7. If I Fell
8. I've Just Seen a Face
9. Lucy in the Sky with Diamonds
10. She Came in Through the Bathroom Window

Exercise 3–D. Manner of articulation: Liquids and Glides

1. Eleanor Rigby
2. Lovely Rita
3. Yellow Submarine
4. Words of Love
5. Young Blood
6. Ballad of John and Yoko
7. Watching Rainbows
8. Winston's Walk
9. Yesterday
10. Run for your Life

Exercise 3–E. Manner of articulation: Affricates

1. Act Naturally
2. Julia
3. Magical Mystery Tour
4. Mother Nature's Son
5. Norwegian Wood
6. Blue Jay Way
7. Baby You're a Rich Man
8. Chains
9. Her Majesty
10. Hey Jude

Chapter 4

/p/ I-M-F Table Transcription Exercise 4–1 AUDIO 1–5

1. [fon]
2. [splɪt]   M
3. [hɪkəp]   F
4. [gofɚ]
5. [ʃapɪŋ]   M
6. [prɛsɪdɛnt]   I
7. [pɛpɚmɪnt]   I & M
8. [numætɪk]

9. [əpɛnd]   M
10. [pæmflɪt]   I

/p/ Transcription Exercise 4–2
AUDIO 1–6

1. [paɪn]
2. [dip]
3. [ə'poz]
4. [kep]
5. ['pepɚ]
6. [sɪp]
7. [ples]
8. [hɛlp]
9. [pæk]

/b/ I-M-F Table Transcription Exercise 4–3
AUDIO 1–7

1. [hʌmbəl]   M
2. [rɪbɪn]   M
3. [bilebɚ]   I & M
4. [pʌblɪk]   M
5. [bɚbæŋk]   I & M
6. [θʌm]
7. [prob]   F
8. [hælɪbʌt]   M
9. [brok]   I
10. [tumston]

/b/ Transcription Exercise 4–4
AUDIO 1–8

1. [bæd]
2. [tʌb]
3. ['bebi]
4. [braɪt]
5. ['ræbɪt]
6. ['nobədi]
7. [bɑm]
8. [kɔb]
9. [kɚb]

/p/ and /b/ Crossword

Across	Down
1. [pɑliwɑg]	1. [pɛbəl]
3. [kʌb]	2. [lipɪŋ]
4. [pʌmps]	
5. [brɪŋ]	

/t/ I-M-F Table Transcription Exercise 4–5
AUDIO 1–9

1. [kɔt]   F
2. [wɪsəl]

3. [tuwɪʃɪn]   I
4. [taɪm]   I
5. [tɛntətɪv]   I & M
6. [tortijə]   I & M
7. [wɑtʃt]   F
8. [ʃæle]
9. [tɛrɪtori]   I & M
10. [moʃən]

/t/ Transcription Exercise 4–6
AUDIO 1–10

1. [tʌb]
2. [kʌt]
3. ['ɪntu]
4. ['ʌntɪl]
5. [twɪn]
6. [kot]
7. ['rotet]
8. [taɪm]
9. [nɛst]

Glottal Stop Transcription Exercise 4–7
AUDIO 1–11

1. ['dulɪtəl]   [dulɪʔl̩]
2. ['mɪtən]   [mɪʔn̩]
3. ['faʊntən]   [faʊn ʔn̩]
4. ['pætənt]   [pæʔn̩t]
5. ['hɪltən]   [hɪlʔn̩]
6. ['bʌtən]   [bʌʔn̩]
7. ['lætən]   [læʔn̩]
8. ['kɔtən]   [kɔʔn̩]
9. ['bɪtən]   [bɪʔn̩]
10. ['moltən]   [molʔn̩]

Voiced /t/ Transcription Exercise 4–8
AUDIO 1–12

1. [bɛ'tɚ]   ['bɛt̬ɚ]
2. [hɔ'tɚ]   ['hɔt̬ɚ]
3. [bæ'təl]   ['bæt̬əl]
4. [mæ'tɚ]   ['mæt̬ɚ]
5. [æ'təm]   ['æt̬əm]
6. [bʌ'tɚ]   ['bʌt̬ɚ]
7. [ke'tɚ]   ['ket̬ɚ]
8. [kwo'tə]   ['kwot̬ə]
9. [tʃi'tɪd]   ['tʃit̬ɪd]
10. [duti]   ['dut̬i]

/d/ I-M-F Table Transcription Exercise 4–9
AUDIO 1–13

1. [hɛdʒ]
2. [hæŋkɚtʃɪf]

3. [mæpt]
4. [dɛdɪnd]   I & M & F
5. [dɛked]   I & F
6. [pɔɪntɛd]   F
7. [ædɪŋ]   M
8. [midijəl]   M
9. [drɛd]   I & F
10. [dimænd]   I & F

/d/ Transcription Exercise 4–10
AUDIO 1–14

1. [do]
2. [ˈkʌndɪʃən]
3. [juzd]
4. [dɪʃ]
5. [ˈmɛdo]
6. [sænd]
7. [dwɛl]
8. [ˈwʌndɚ]
9. [ˈtʃɛndʒd]

/t/ and /d/ Crossword Puzzle

Across
1. [dɛf]
2. [dɪziz]
3. [detə]

Down
1. [daɪmz]
2. [dituɚ]
3. [dɑt]

/k/ I-M-F Table Transcription Exercise 4–11
AUDIO 1–15

1. [sɛntɪmitɚ]
2. [pike]   M
3. [kwortɛt]   I
4. [tɛkst]   M
5. [braŋkaɪtɪs]   M
6. [ɪmpɛkəbəl]   M
7. [krɪtɪk]   I & F
8. [bækek]   M & F
9. [naɪt]
10. [tokvɪl]   M

/k/ Transcription Exercise 4–12
AUDIO 1–16

1. [bæk]
2. [kaʊnt]
3. [tɪk]
4. [ˈbæskɪt]
5. [kek]
6. [krim]
7. [ˈstakɪŋ]
8. [əˈkras]
9. [marˈki]

/g/ I-M-F Table Transcription Exercise 4–13
AUDIO 1–17

1. [dʒɛntəl]
2. [garbɪdʒ]   I
3. [næt]
4. [ɛgnag]   M & F
5. [ɛgzɪst]   M
6. [gaʊdʒ]   I
7. [læf]
8. [gɝtrud]   I
9. [lɪŋgɚ]   M
10. [dɪdʒɪt]

/g/ Transcription Exercise 4–14
AUDIO 1–18

1. [gan]
2. [ˈwɪgəl]
3. [ˈhʌŋgri]
4. [bɛg]
5. [dɔg]
6. [grin]
7. [veg]
8. [glʌv]
9. [ˈgrɪdəl]

/k/ and /g/ Crossword Puzzle

Across
2. [ʃʊgɚ]
3. [brɛkfɛst]
5. [kɔfi]
6. [næpkɪn]

Down
1. [jogɚt]
3. [bekən]
4. [ɛgz]

Stop-Consonant Transcription Exercise 4–15
AUDIO 1–19

1. [ˈpɝpɪtret]
2. [ˈbʌkɪt]
3. [ˈklepat]
4. [drapt]
5. [pop]
6. [datudat]
7. [ˈkʌpkek]
8. [ˈbebid]
9. [ˈdɛdbolt]
10. [kot]
11. [ˈpʌgodə]
12. [ˈbɝdbik]
13. [frɪkst]
14. [ˈlæptap]
15. [ˈgæbi]
16. [ˈdagtæg]
17. [bækʌp]
18. [ˈtogə]
19. [pɔkɪtbʊk]
20. [kɛpt]

Chapter 5

/m/ I-M-F Table Transcription Exercise 5–1
AUDIO 1–20

1. [mɝmed]   I & M
2. [daɪm]   F

3. [pɑm]   F
4. [mʌm]   I & F
5. [kæzəm]   F
6. [mɪnɪmʌm]   I & M & F
7. [mɛmbren]   I & M
8. [hæmɚ]   M
9. [skwɚm]   F
10. [ɛmpɑɪjɚ]   M

/m/ Transcription Exercise 5–2
AUDIO 1–21

1. [mɑɪt]
2. [læmp]
3. [mit]
4. [tim]
5. ['kæmɚə]
6. [mɑlt]
7. ['rændəm]
8. [hɑrm]
9. [smɛl]

/n/ I-M-F Table Transcription Exercise 5–3
AUDIO 1–22

1. [næpsæk]   I
2. [kɛnəl]   M
3. [nɑnsɛnᵗs]   I & M
4. [zon]   F
5. [næʃ]   I
6. [numæᵗɪk]   I
7. [nun]   I & F
8. [nom]   I
9. [bɪgɪnɚ]   M
10. [sɛvɪntin]   F

/n/ Transcription Exercise 5–4
AUDIO 1–23

1. ['tɛnɪs]
2. ['kæbɪn]
3. ['nɔɪzi]
4. ['kʌnɛri]
5. ['nɑtɪkəl]
6. ['vɑɪolɪn]
7. ['hændi]
8. ['pænəl]
9. ['nɑɪlɑn]

/ŋ/ I-M-F Table Transcription Exercise 5–5
AUDIO 1–24

1. [mʌŋki]   M
2. [sɪŋɪŋ]   M & F
3. [kɪŋdʌm]   M
4. [ʌrendʒ]

5. [ilɑŋget]   M
6. [rɔŋ]   F
7. [dʒɪŋgəl]   M
8. [lɛŋkθ]   M
9. [feŋz]   M
10. [spʌndʒ]

/ŋ/ Transcription Exercise 5–6
AUDIO 1–25

1. ['bɔŋgo]
2. ['strɑŋgli]
3. ['hɑŋkɑŋ]
4. [wɪŋ]
5. [tʌŋ]
6. ['ʃɪŋgəl]
7. ['dɑɪnɪŋ]
8. [feŋ]
9. ['sevɪŋz]

/m/ /n/ and /ŋ/ Crossword Puzzle

Across
1. [nɑɪn]
3. [kɪŋdəm]
4. [numonjə]

Down
1. [næpkɪn]
2. [stim]

Nasal Consonant Transcription Exercise 5–7
AUDIO 1–26

1. ['nezəl]
2. ['mɑnjumɛntəl]
3. [ə'mʌŋ]
4. ['rɛmnɪnt]
5. [nɑmɪnet]
6. ['fɛmɪnɪn]
7. ['lɛmoned]
8. ['mornɪŋ]
9. ['tʃɪmni]
10. [mi'tɪŋ]
11. ['kʌntenɪŋ]
12. ['mɪŋglɪŋ]
13. ['mɛmbren]
14. ['mʌni]
15. ['næni]
16. ['mɝeŋ]
17. ['mɑʊntɪn]
18. ['numɛrɪkəl]
19. [sɪnə'mʌn]
20. ['munbim]

Transcription Exercise 5–8
AUDIO 1–27

		Formal Speech	Casual Speech
1.	cabin	[kæbɪn]	[kæbm̩]
2.	medal	[mɛdəl]	[mɛdl̩]
3.	redden	[rɛdɪn]	[rɛdn̩]
4.	ribbon	[rɪbɪn]	[rɪbm̩]
5.	blacken	[blækɪn]	[blækŋ̩]
6.	panel	[pænəl]	[pænl̩]
7.	milking	[mɪlkɪŋ]	[mɪlkŋ̩]
8.	garden	[gɑrdɪn]	[gɑrdn̩]
9.	broken	[brokɪn]	[brokŋ̩]
10.	open	[opɪn]	[opm̩]

Chapter 6

/f/ I-M-F Table Transcription Exercise 6–1
AUDIO 1–28

1. [fɑsforəs]   I & M
2. [pæmflɪt]   M
3. [dʒɝæf]   F
4. [foto]   I
5. [fɪftin]   I & M
6. [dʒosɪf]   F
7. [sfɪrɪkəl]   M
8. [mɑnogræf]   F
9. [flʌfi]   I & M
10. [fonəgræf]   I & F

/f/ Transcription Exercise 6–2
AUDIO 1–29

1. [fʌn]
2. [bɪ'for]
3. ['fɪftin]
4. [frɑst]
5. ['kɔfi]
6. [lif]
7. [læf]
8. [flot]
9. [ɪf]

/v/ I-M-F Table Transcription Exercise 6–3
AUDIO 1–30

1. [vɪndɪktɪv]   I & F
2. [waɪf]
3. [ʃɛvrɑn]   M
4. [wivɝ]   F
5. [ʌv]   F
6. [laɪfsevɪŋ]   M
7. [nɛvɝ]   M
8. [waɪvz]   M
9. [vɛrɪfaɪ]   I
10. [stov]   F

/v/ Transcription Exercise 6–4
AUDIO 1–31

1. [vaɪn]
2. ['vɛlvɪt]
3. ['ovɝ]
4. ['vɛri]
5. ['ɪnvaɪt]
6. [lɪv]
7. ['vælju]
8. [wivɝ]
9. [muv]

/f/ and /v/ Crossword Puzzle

Across	Down
1. [kæfin]	1. [kævɪti]
4. [ves]	2. [fɛstɪvəl]
5. [flɪp]	3. [notɪfaɪ]

/s/ I-M-F Table Transcription Exercise 6–5
AUDIO 1–32

1. [sɪti]   I
2. [ʃevz]
3. [disɛptɪv]   M
4. [blɪnts]   F
5. [juʒul]
6. [æksɪz]   M
7. [breslɪt]   M
8. [aɪlɪnd]
9. [sudo]   I
10. [brɑŋks]   F

/s/ Transcription Exercise 6–6
AUDIO 1–33

1. [ɛls]
2. [ə'slip]
3. [su'pirijɝ]
4. ['besɪn]
5. ['istɝ]
6. ['sidɝ]
7. [æsks]
8. ['sændəl]
9. [blæst]

/z/ I-M-F Table Transcription Exercise 6–7
AUDIO 1–34

1. [kɪdz]   F
2. [zɑr]   I
3. [tʃiz]   F
4. [ɑbzɝv]   M
5. [bɪznɪs]   M
6. [nɑzəl]   M
7. [prɛzɪnt]   M
8. [ɪz]   F
9. [siʒɝ]
10. [bɑbslɛdz]   F

/z/ Transcription Exercise 6–8
AUDIO 1–35

1. ['bɪzi]
2. ['vɪzɪt]
3. ['zɝkɑn]
4. ['wizəl]
5. [siz]

6. ['zɪnijə]
7. [ðoz]
8. ['zukini]
9. [gɪvz]

/s/ and /z/ Crossword Puzzle

Across
3. [zɪp]
4. [sɪzəl]
5. [soldʒɚ]

Down
1. [sups]
2. [zil]
3. [zoro]
5. [sizənz]

Fricative Consonant Transcription
Exercise 6–9
AUDIO 1–37

1. ['fɛstɪv]
2. [swɪs]
3. ['vɛsəl]
4. ['fænsɪfʊl]
5. ['mizəlz]
6. [zɛst]
7. ['vɪvɪd]
8. ['ɛkspɛnsɪv]
9. ['bɪznɪsɪz]
10. [forˈgɪv]
11. ['sopsʌdz]
12. ['fæsɪn]
13. [skwiz]
14. ['sɪzɚz]
15. ['farməsi]
16. ['stivɪn]
17. [vaɪs]
18. ['swɪtzɚlænd]
19. [sefˈtɪ]
20. [sɪˈvɪljən]

/θ/ I-M-F Table Transcription Exercise 6–10
AUDIO 1–38

1. [ɛnθuzijæst] M
2. [θɚzde] I
3. [θɚðɚ] I
4. [ilɪzʌbɛθ] F
5. [θɚˈtiθɚd] I & M
6. [gaθɪk] M
7. [kʌθidrəl] M
8. [θru] I
9. [ænʌsθiʒʌ] M
10. [zinɪθ] F

/θ/ Transcription Exercise 6–11
AUDIO 1–39

1. [θɪn]
2. ['bɚθde]
3. [wɪdθ]
4. [tiθ]
5. [θro]
6. ['ɪniθɪŋ]
7. [norθ]
8. ['nʌθɪŋ]
9. [θɔ]

/ð/ I-M-F Table Transcription Exercise 6–12
AUDIO 1–40

1. [ðɛm] I
2. [kloð] F
3. [hɛðɚ] M
4. [rɪðəm] M
5. [tiθ]
6. [norθ]
7. [wɛðɚ] M
8. [θaɪ]
9. [norðɚn] M
10. [wɛðɚ] M

/ð/ Transcription Exercise 6–13
AUDIO 1–41

1. [ðɪs]
2. ['iðɚ]
3. [ðɛr]
4. ['faðɚ]
5. [sɪð]
6. [ðo]
7. ['mʌðɚ]
8. [tɪð]
9. [smuð]

"th" Transcription Exercise 6–14
AUDIO 1–42

1. ð	11. ð	21. θ
2. ð	12. ð	22. θ
3. θ	13. θ	23. θ
4. θ	14. ð	24. ð
5. ð	15. ð	25. θ
6. ð	16. θ	26. ð
7. θ	17. ð	27. ð
8. ð	18. ð	28. ð
9. θ	19. ð	29. ð
10. ð	20. θ	30. θ

/θ/ and /ð/ Crossword Puzzle

Across
1. [faðɚ]
2. [ðoz]
3. [mʌðɚz]
4. [θɪn]
6. [rɪðəm]

Down
1. [fɛðɚz]
3. [mɛθadɪk]
5. [norθ]

Interdental Consonant Transcription
Exercise 6–15
AUDIO 1–43

1. [baɪkˈʌθɔn]
2. [wadzˈwɚθ]
3. [saʊθistɚn]
4. ['ʌrɪθmətɪk]

5. [sɛvəntinθ]
6. [ˈθrɛtɪn]
7. [ʌndɚgroθ]
8. [sʌðɚnmost]
9. [θʌndɚbɝd]
10. [ˈplɪməθ]
11. [ruθlɛsli]
12. [wɪðɚspun]

13. [ˈhɑrtθrab]
14. [ˈwɝði]
15. [θraɪvɪŋ]
16. [ənˈʌðɚ]
17. [mɛθadɪk]
18. [ˈθaʔlɛs]
19. [ˈhʌndrɛθ]
20. [ˈlɛðɚ]

/h/ I-M-F Table Transcription Exercise 6–16
AUDIO 1–44

1. [hum]   I
2. [rihɚs]   M
3. [hɪtʃhaɪk]   I & M
4. [ʌnholsəm]   M
5. [hoze]   I
6. [ɪnhel]   M
7. [hɪləmanstɚ]   I
8. [hæbɪtæt]   I
9. [mʌhagəni]   M
10. [ɛkshəleʃən]   M

/h/ Transcription Exercise 6–17
AUDIO 1–45

1. [hɛft]
2. [ˈharbɚ]
3. [moˈhɛr]
4. [ˈʌphɪl]
5. [hʌm]
6. [ˈɪnhɛrɪt]
7. [ˈrihɚs]
8. [ˈhɝmɪt]
9. [ˈʌnhʊk]

/ʍ/ I-M-F Table Transcription Exercise 6–18
AUDIO 1–46

1. [ʍil]   I
2. [kʍin]   M
3. [sʍɛr]   M
4. [ʍaɪ]   I
5. [sʍed]   M
6. [ʍɛr]   I
7. [holʍit]   M
8. [wɛr]
9. [wægɪn]
10. [skʍɛr]   M

/ʍ/ Transcription Exercise 6–19
AUDIO 1–47

1. [ʍɪm]
2. [ˈovɚʍɛlm]

3. [ʍɪp]
4. [ˈtʍɛntɪ]
5. [ʃʍa]
6. [ʍaɪt]
7. [ˈsʌmʍɛr]
8. [ˈmɛðɚ]
9. [ʍorf]

/h/ and /hw/ Transcription Exercise 6–20
AUDIO 1–48

1. [ˈhɛdʒhag]   11. [hu]
2. [sʍed]   12. [ˈʍæmɪ]
3. [ʍɝl]   13. [holharˈtɪd]
4. [hum]   14. [ʍɛr]
5. [sʍe]   15. [ˈpɪnʍil]
6. [ˈwɑhu]   16. [hɪm]
7. [ʍaɪn]   17. [ˈpɝsʍed]
8. [hændˈʃek]   18. [ʍɪsəl]
9. [hɛr]   19. [ohaɪo]
10. [ʍɪf]   20. [huz]

/ʃ/ I-M-F Table Transcription Exercise 6–21
AUDIO 1–49

1. [kʌndɪʃən]   M
2. [ʌʃɚ]   M
3. [tɪʃju]   M
4. [broʃɚ]   M
5. [ʃɪfan]   I
6. [ɪnɪʃəl]   M
7. [trɛʒɚ]
8. [lɪkorɪʃ]   F
9. [krieʃən]   M
10. [ʃubrʌʃ]   I & F

/ʃ/ Transcription Exercise 6–22
AUDIO 1–50

1. [ʃu]
2. [ˈmʌstæʃ]
3. [ˈoʃən]
4. [ˈɪnʃɚ]
5. [wɪʃ]
6. [ʃɪp]
7. [ˈrɛlɪʃ]
8. [ʃek]
9. [ˈfæʃən]

/ʒ/ I-M-F Table Transcription Exercise 6–23
AUDIO 1–51

1. [vɪʒɪn]   M
2. [ʌfeʒə]   M
3. [gʌrɑʒ]   F

4. [stefən]
5. [trɛʒɚ]   M
6. [pɝʒə]   M
7. [kloʒɚ]   M
8. [ruʒ]   F
9. [kʌmpoʒɚ]   M
10. [tɛləvɪʒən]   M

/ʒ/ Transcription Exercise 6–24
AUDIO 1–52

1. ['rɛʒim]
2. [loʒ]
3. ['plɛʒɚ]
4. ['dɪvɪʒɪn]
5. ['juʒjuəl]
6. ['kʌlɪʒɪn]
7. [beʒ]
8. ['kolɑʒ]
9. [kæʒjul]

/ʃ/ and /ʒ/ Crossword Puzzle

Across   Down
1. [vekeʃən]   2. [kʌlɪwən]
3. [liʒɚ]   5. [fɪʃ]
4. [ʌfeʒə]
6. [ʃʌn]

Chapter 7

/tʃ/ I-M-F Table Transcription Exercise 7–1
AUDIO 1–53

1. [ʃɛf]
2. [hætʃɪt]   M
3. [pɪtʃ]   F
4. [broʃɚ]
5. [kord]
6. [kʌltʃɚ]   M
7. [ek]
8. [mʌʃin]
9. [tʃɝtʃ]   I & F
10. [fjutʃɚ]   M

/tʃ/ Transcription Exercise 7–2
AUDIO 1–54

1. [tʃɪn]
2. ['pitʃɪz]
3. [wɪtʃ]
4. [tʃiz]
5. [lʌntʃ]
6. ['titʃɚ]

7. ['tʃɪldrɛn]
8. [skatʃ]
9. ['fɝnətʃɚ]

/dʒ/ I-M-F Table Transcription Exercise 7–3
AUDIO 1–55

1. [gʌrɑdʒ]   F
2. [bʌdʒɪt]   M
3. [dʒɪndʒɚ]   I & M
4. [dʌndʒən]   M
5. [dʒʌmp]   I
6. [ɛdʒjukeʃən]   M
7. [dʒɛstʃɚ]   I
8. [vɔɪjɪdʒ]   F
9. ['ɪndʒɪn]   M
10. [splɝdʒ]   F

/dʒ/ Transcription Exercise 7–4
AUDIO 1–56

1. [dʒʌŋk]
2. [ɛn'dʒɔɪ]
3. [ɝdʒd]
4. ['vɪdʒəl]
5. [wedʒ]
6. [dʒɛm]
7. ['dʒʌmbo]
8. ['kɑlədʒɪn]
9. [fʌdʒ]

/tʃ/ and /dʒ/ Crossword Puzzle

Across   Down
2. [endʒəlz]   1. [klɝdʒi]
3. [ridʒɔɪs]   4. [sɑmz]
5. [pritʃɚz]

Fricative and Affricate Consonant Transcription Exercise 7–5
AUDIO 1–57

1. ['ʃuʃaɪn]   11. ['stedʒkotʃ]
2. ['daɪdʒɛstʃən]   12. ['tʃaɪldɪʃ]
3. ['kʌnfjuʒɪn]   13. ['hɑdʒpɑdʒ]
4. ['ɑntɝɑʒ]   14. [pɛriʒən]
5. [ægrɪ'kʌltʃɚ]   15. ['sʌgdʒɛstʃən]
6. [vaɪ'veʃəs]   16. ['tʃɪntʃɪlə]
7. ['sæbətɑʒ]   17. [kolɛkʃən]
8. [ɛn'tʃæntɪd]   18. [fortʃənɪt]
9. [dʒek]   19. [bjutɪʃən]
10. [ʃɪptuʃor]   20. [vɪʒjulaɪz]

Chapter 8

/w/ I-M-F Table Transcription Exercise 8–1
AUDIO 1–58

1. [wʌnts]	I
2. [wɪdo]	I
3. [gwɑm]	M
4. [twaɪs]	M
5. [ɪgwɑnə]	M
6. [ʍɛr]	
7. [kiwi]	M
8. [kʍɛstʃɪn]	
9. [wɪlo]	I
10. [eŋgwɪʃ]	M

/w/ Transcription Exercise 8–2
AUDIO 1–59

1. [wæks]
2. ['dʒægwɑr]
3. [bi'wɛr]
4. [swɛl]
5. ['wʌndɚ]
6. [kwin]
7. ['forwɚd]
8. [twɪn]
9. [wɛt]

/j/ I-M-F Table Transcription Exercise 8–3
AUDIO 1–60

1. [ɪndʒɛkt]	
2. [rɔɪjəl]	M
3. [jɛt]	I
4. [zɪljən]	M
5. [bʌnjən]	M
6. [spænjəl]	M
7. [jojo]	I & M
8. [lejɛt]	M
9. [fɪgjɚ]	M
10. [kaɪjoti]	M

/j/ Transcription Exercise 8–4
AUDIO 1–61

1. [jor]
2. [bi'jand]
3. [jild]
4. [pʌ'paɪjə]
5. ['jandɚ]
6. [fʌmɪljɚ]
7. [jɑrn]
8. ['bɪljʌn]
9. [jɛs]

/l/ I-M-F Table Transcription Exercise 8–5
AUDIO 1–62

1. [mɔl]	F
2. [lɪnolijəm]	I & M
3. [wel]	F
4. [æpəl]	F
5. [fɛlo]	M
6. [kævz]	
7. [lʌləbaɪ]	I & M
8. [flotɪlə]	M
9. [hɛlm]	M
10. [soʃəbəl]	F

/l/ Transcription Exercise 8–6
AUDIO 1–63

1. ['lʌki]
2. ['lɛmən]
3. [klaʊn]
4. ['sændəl]
5. ['goldən]
6. [ɛls]
7. ['braɪdəl]
8. [fli]
9. ['liɑn]

/r/ I-M-F Table Transcription Exercise 8–7
AUDIO 1–64

1. [ræp]	I
2. [raɪ]	I
3. [skɑr]	F
4. [riport]	I & M
5. [rʌbɚ]	M
6. [wordrob]	M
7. [raɪ]	I
8. [gɑrdɪn]	M
9. [bifor]	F
10. [dir]	F

/r/ Transcription Exercise 8–8
AUDIO 1–65

1. [raɪt]
2. [ɪm'prɛs]
3. [ri'dus]
4. ['sɑri]
5. [raɪm]
6. ['ɔlrɛdi]
7. [tʃɛr]
8. [rʌb]
9. [bɑr]

/ir/ I-M-F Table Transcription Exercise 8–9
AUDIO 1–66

1. [spir]   F
2. [wird]   M
3. [siriz]   M
4. [stir]   F
5. [pɛr]
6. [firs]   M
7. [irb]   I
8. [kʌrir]   F
9. [mɝθ]
10. [waɪjɚ]

/ɛr/ I-M-F Table Transcription Exercise 8–10
AUDIO 1–67

1. [stɛr]   F
2. [skwɛr]   F
3. [bɛrəl]   M
4. [wɛr]   F
5. [trelɚ]
6. [stɛr]   F
7. [pɝl]
8. [tʃɛr]   F
9. [bɛr]   F
10. [kɛrəmɛl] M

/ar/ I-M-F Table Transcription Exercise 8–11
AUDIO 1–68

1. [hart]   M
2. [star]   F
3. [sardʒɪnt] M
4. [fars]   M
5. [kɛrɪdʒ]
6. [stɛr]
7. [mɛri]
8. [mʌrin]
9. [parti]   M
10. [karbʌn] M

/or/ I-M-F Table Transcription Exercise 8–12
AUDIO 1–69

1. [forθ]   M
2. [kʌort]   M
3. [parlɚ]
4. [worf]   M
5. [sor]   F
6. [wort]   M
7. [rumɚ]
8. [kort]   M
9. [por]   F
10. [wɝld]

/j/, /l/, and /r/ Crossword Puzzle

Across	Down
2. [jɛlo]	1. [til]
4. [roz]	3. [orɪndʒ]
5. [dʒʌŋgəlgrin]	6. [lævɪndɚ]
7. [vaɪolɛt]	
8. [mərun]	

Vowel plus r Transcription Exercise 8–13
AUDIO 1–70

1. ['irmark]   11. [spars]
2. ['kɛrworn]   12. ['ardvark]
3. [or]   13. [dʒir]
4. [spirz]   14. [bor]
5. ['karport]   15. ['forskʍɛr]
6. [ʃir]   16. [fars]
7. ['hardwɛr]   17. [kors]
8. [dart]   18. [smirz]
9. [for'lorn]   19. [startʃ]
10. [rɛr]   20. [bɛr]

Oral Resonant Consonant Transcription Exercise 8–14
AUDIO 1–71

1. [jok]   11. ['redijetɚ]
2. [dworf]   12. ['kʍaɪjɪtli]
3. ['liwe]   13. [væljɛnt]
4. ['domɪnjʌn]   14. ['frikʍɛntsi]
5. ['kʍɪbəl]   15. ['lɔɪjɚ]
6. ['larsɪni]   16. ['wewɚd]
7. ['jɝenijəm]   17. ['jolandʌ]
8. [ɪləstret]   18. ['stæljʌnz]
9. ['ræli]   19. ['rɛsəl]
10. ['sɔɪjɚ]   20. [jɔn]

Chapter 10

/i/ I-M-F Table Transcription Exercise 10–1
AUDIO 2–1

1. [jɛs]
2. [livɪŋ]   M
3. [il]   I
4. [θivz]   M
5. [pipəl]   M
6. [tʃipɪn]   M
7. [kiʃ]   M
8. [strit]   M
9. [hilɪks]   M
10. [haɪjɚ]

/i/ Transcription Exercise 10–2
AUDIO 2–2

1. [it]
2. [kip]
3. [did]
4. [ki]
5. [bik]
6. [pik]
7. [bit]
8. [ti]
9. [dip]

/ɪ/ I-M-F Table Transcription Exercise 10–3
AUDIO 2–3

1. [maɪld]	
2. [ɪt]	I
3. [pɪksi]	M
4. [bɪljən]	M
5. [faɪn]	
6. [gɪlt]	M
7. [vɪlɪn]	M
8. [sɪnsiɚ]	M
9. [lɪmᵖf]	M
10. [fɪn]	M

/ɪ/ Transcription Exercise 10–4
AUDIO 2–4

1. [kɪk]
2. [gɪg]
3. [bɪld]
4. [tɪk]
5. [ɪt]
6. [bɪt]
7. [pɪk]
8. [kɪd]
9. [bɪg]

/ɛ/ I-M-F Table Transcription Exercise 10–5
AUDIO 2–5

1. [ɛntel]	I
2. [pɛŋgwɪn]	M
3. [bɛl]	M
4. [maɪld]	
5. [jɛs]	M
6. [ɛlf]	I
7. [gæŋ]	
8. [ɛθɪk]	I
9. [gɛs]	M
10. [dʒɛləs]	M

/ɛ/ Transcription Exercise 10–6
AUDIO 2–6

1. [mɛld]
2. [ɛnd]
3. [dɛl]
4. [dɛn]
5. [lɛd]
6. [nɛl]
7. [dɛnts]
8. [slɛd]
9. [ɛtʃ]

/e/ I-M-F Table Transcription Exercise 10–7
AUDIO 2–7

1. [ekorn]	I
2. [sle]	F
3. [ven]	M
4. [daɪl]	
5. [liʒɚ]	
6. [gen]	M
7. [bæg]	
8. [le]	F
9. [əten]	M
10. [rendir]	M

/e/ Transcription Exercise 10–8
AUDIO 2–8

1. [ves]
2. [stez]
3. [zen]
4. [et]
5. [fez]
6. [test]
7. [fes]
8. [ʃev]
9. [fet]

/æ/ I-M-F Table Transcription Exercise 10–9
AUDIO 2–9

1. [ædvænts]	I & M
2. [pæn]	M
3. [ænt]	I
4. [mɑl]	
5. [pen]	
6. [dæmpnɪs]	M
7. [kwæk]	M
8. [kæsked]	M
9. [mæθ]	M
10. [wɛnt]	

/æ/ Transcription Exercise 10–10
AUDIO 2–10

1. [sæ∫]
2. [fæst]
3. [æ∫]
4. [stæf]
5. [væt]
6. [∫æft]
7. [tæt]
8. [æz]
9. [sæv]

/i/, /ɪ/, /ɛ/, /e/, /æ/, and /w/ Crossword Puzzle

Across	Down
1. [wɛbstɚ]	1. [wɪn]
2. [wɪnstʌn]	2. [wɪljʌm]
4. [len]	3. [tɪm]
5. [mɛri]	6. [∫ilʌ]

Front Vowel Transcription Exercise 10–11
AUDIO 2–11

1. [flem]	11. ['dʒɪmnɪst]
2. ['æli]	12. ['eprɪn]
3. [bi'liv]	13. ['nemsek]
4. [re'zɪn]	14. ['bɪzi]
5. [wik'de]	15. ['kæfin]
6. ['rilæks]	16. ['wɪmɪn]
7. [æsk]	17. ['hɛdek]
8. ['pipəl]	18. [pliz]
9. [rɛmnɪnt]	19. ['bɪskɪt]
10. [ren]	20. ['ɛldɪst]

Chapter 11

/ə/ I-M-F Table Transcription Exercise 11–1
AUDIO 2–12

1. [əhɛd]   I
2. [rətæn]   M
3. [mə∫in]   M
4. [bətan]   M
5. [kʌbanə]   F
6. [tubə]   F
7. [vænɪlə]   F
8. [əgri]   I
9. [bəfe]   M
10. [kəkun]   M

/ə/ Transcription Exercise 11–2
AUDIO 2–13

1. [gə'lor]
2. [sə'port]

3. [ə'lon]
4. [kəm'poz]
5. [kən'don]
6. [pə'trol]
7. [rə'por]
8. [ə'∫or]
9. [lə'gun]

/ə/ Crossword Puzzle

Across	Down
4. [səpoz]	1. [pəpus]
5. [kəkun]	2. [gəzəl]
6. [ləgun]	3. [əpan]

/ʌ/ I-M-F Table Transcription Exercise 11–3
AUDIO 2–14

1. [ʌv]   I
2. [t∫ʌg]   M
3. [wʌn]   M
4. [ʌnkʌt]   I & M
5. [wʌz]   M
6. [jʌŋ]   M
7. [rʌst]   M
8. [ʌp]   I
9. [wʌn]   M
10. [rust]

/ʌ/ Transcription Exercise 11–4
AUDIO 2–15

1. [ʌvin]
2. [tʌt∫]
3. [θʌm]
4. [bʌm]
5. [tʌn]
6. [pʌn]
7. [mʌt]
8. [kʌd]
9. [nʌt]

/ʌ/ Crossword Puzzle

Across	Down
3. [ʌnglud]	1. [dʌst]
6. [∫ʌt]	2. [hʌ∫]
	4. [gʌmbo]
	5. [dʌk]

/ɚ/ I-M-F Table Transcription Exercise 11–5
AUDIO 2–16

1. [æktɚ]   F
2. [ɝnɚ]   F
3. [nɝd]

4. [ʃʊgɚ]   F
5. [eŋgɚ]   F
6. [nebɚ]   F
7. [kritʃɚ]   F
8. [kɚtɪn]
9. [glæmɚ]   F
10. [pepɚ]   F

/ɚ/ Transcription Exercises 11–6
AUDIO 2–17

1. ['netʃɚ]
2. ['medʒɚ]
3. ['bekɚ]
4. ['rezɚ]
5. ['letɚ]
6. ['pesɚ]
7. ['feljɚ]
8. ['nebɚ]
9. ['sefɚ]

/ɚ/ Crossword Puzzle

Across   Down
3. [flaʊwɚ]   1. [ɛvɚ]
4. [læntɚn]   2. [ɛfɚt]
                4. [lidɚ]
                5. [nɛvɚ]

/ɝ/ I-M-F Table Transcription Exercise 11–7
AUDIO 2–18

1. [ɝb]   I
2. [wɝst]   M
3. [slɝ]   F
4. [tʃɝp]   M
5. [sɝdʒɪn]   M
6. [ɝn]   I
7. [pɝtʃəs]   M
8. [ɝn]   I
9. [tɝtəl]   M
10. [mɝtəl]   M

/ɝ/ Transcription Exercise 11–8
AUDIO 2–19

1. [ɝdʒ]
2. [vɝb]
3. [bɝθ]
4. [θɝd]
5. [dɝdʒ]
6. [bɝ]
7. [gɝθ]
8. [dʒɝm]
9. [ɝθ]

/ɝ/ Crossword Puzzle

Across   Down
2. [ɝbəl]   1. [bɝst]
4. [θɝsti]   3. [zɝkan]
6. [nɝsmed]   5. [θɝd]

Central Vowels Transcription Exercise 11–9
AUDIO 2–20

1. [hæmbɚgɚ]   11. ['tɝnɚ]
2. [sʌdz]   12. [kʌn'fɝm]
3. [kɝn]   13. ['bʌzɚ]
4. ['kʌvɚ]   14. ['mʌtʃɚ]
5. [ʌ'kɚ]   15. ['bʌfɚ]
6. ['fɝvɚ]   16. [tʃɝp]
7. ['ʌndʌn]   17. [sɝdʒ]
8. ['irdrʌm]   18. [vɝs]
9. ['mɝmɚ]   19. [sʌb'mɝdʒ]
10. [ə'waɪl]   20. ['mɝdʒɚ]

/ə/ Transcription Exercise 11–11
AUDIO 2–22

1. cousin   cousin   ['kʌzən]
2. illness illness ['ɪlnəs]
3. distant distant ['dɪstənt]
4. promise promise ['praməs]
5. palace   palace   ['pæləs]
6. socket   socket   ['sakət]
7. disease disease ['dəziz]
8. escape   escape   ['əskep]
9. contain contain [kən'ten]
10. divide divide   [də'vaɪd]

/ʌ/ Transcription Exercise 11–12
AUDIO 2–23

1. gulf   [gʌlf]
2. dust   [dʌst]
3. dumb   [dʌm]
4. fuzz   [fʌz]
5. putt   [pʌt]
6. plus   [plʌs]
7. lug   [lʌg]
8. stuck   [stʌk]
9. crumb   [krʌm]
10. plum   [plʌm]

/ɝ/ Transcription Exercise 11–13
AUDIO 2–24

1. clerk   [klɝk]
2. first   [fɝst]
3. heard   [hɝd]
4. fur   [fɝ]

5. cursed   [kɝst]
6. shirk   [ʃɝk]
7. were   [wɝ]
8. whirl   [wɝl]
9. per   [pɝ]
10. curl   [kɝl]

3. [lus]
4. [ru]
5. [lup]
6. [flu]
7. [slup]
8. [pul]
9. [ful]

/ʌ/ɝ/ Transcription Exercise 11–14
AUDIO 2–25

1. bun	[bʌn]	burn	[bɝn]
2. shuck	[ʃʌk]	shirk	[ʃɝk]
3. buzz	[bʌz]	burns	[bɝnz]
4. hut	[hʌt]	hurt	[hɝt]
5. shut	[ʃʌt]	shirt	[ʃɝt]
6. cut	[kʌt]	curt	[kɝt]
7. luck	[lʌk]	lurk	[lɝk]
8. putt	[pʌt]	pert	[pɝt]
9. bust	[bʌst]	burst	[bɝst]
10. hub	[hʌb]	Herb	[hɝb]

/ɚ/ Transcription Exercise 11–15
AUDIO 2–26

1. plumber   ['plʌmɚ]
2. other   ['ʌðɚ]
3. cluster   ['klʌstɚ]
4. ulcer   ['ʌlsɚ]
5. buffer   ['bʌfɚ]
6. butler   ['bʌtlɚ]
7. plunger   ['plʌndʒɚ]
8. rubber   ['rʌbɚ]
9. southern   ['sʌðɚn]
10. sculpture   ['skʌlptʃɚ]

Chapter 12

/u/ I-M-F Table Transcription Exercise 12–1
AUDIO 2–27

1. [nudəl]   M
2. [du]   F
3. [du]   F
4. [ʃʊd]
5. [uz]   I
6. [sut]   M
7. [butik]   M
8. [ful]   M
9. [duk]   M
10. [tu]   F

/u/ Transcription Exercise 12–2
AUDIO 2–28

1. [rul]
2. [su]

/ʊ/ I-M-F Table Transcription Exercise 12–3
AUDIO 2–29

1. [fʊl]   M
2. [ʊps]   I
3. [wʊlf]   M
4. [mʌt]
5. [sʊt]   M
6. [guf]
7. [wʊps]   M
8. [ʃʊgɚ]   M
9. [fʊtstul]   M
10. [hʊd]   M

/ʊ/ Transcription Exercise 12–4
AUDIO 2–30

1. [kʊk]
2. [wʊl]
3. [fʊt]
4. [wʊd]
5. [lʊk]
6. [wʊlf]
7. [fʊl]
8. [kʊd]
9. [nʊk]

/o/ I-M-F Table Transcription Exercise 12–5
AUDIO 2–31

1. [old]   I
2. [mut]
3. [so]   F
4. [loʃən]   M
5. [mo]   F
6. [hu]
7. [kolə]   M
8. [tost]   M
9. [bol]   M
10. [mɑtʃo]   F

/o/ Transcription Exercise 12–6
AUDIO 2–32

1. [not]
2. [ton]
3. [on]
4. [tot]

5. [no]
6. [ot]
7. [hon]
8. [no]
9. [o]

/ɔ/ I-M-F Table Transcription Exercise 12–7
AUDIO 2–33

1. [ɔl]   I
2. [θɔŋ]   M
3. [sɔs]   M
4. [ɔ]   I
5. [ʃwɔ]   F
6. [mɔθ]   M
7. [pɔ]   F
8. [skwɔ]   F
9. [pɔ]   F
10. [θɔt]   M

/ɔ/ Transcription Exercise 12–8
AUDIO 2–34

1. [sɔt]
2. ['bɔdi]
3. [rɔt]
4. [prɔn]
5. [kɔl]
6. [tɔt]
7. [θɔt]
8. [vɔlt]
9. [lɔfʊl]

/ɑ/ I-M-F Table Transcription Exercise 12–9
AUDIO 2–35

1. [pɑsţə]   M
2. [ɑmənd]   I
3. [spɑ]   F
4. [lɑntʃ]   M
5. [wɑnrə]   M
6. [jɑt]   M
7. [ɑkwə]   I
8. [lʌntʃ]
9. [ʃwɑ]   F
10. [ɑntre]   I

/ɑ/ Transcription Exercise 12–10
AUDIO 2–36

1. [ɑ]
2. [nɑt]
3. [hɑ]
4. [jɑt]
5. [tɑt]

6. [jɑn]
7. [hɑnt]
8. [tɑt]
9. [ɑnt]

/u/, /ʊ/, /o/, /ɔ/, and /ɑ/ Crossword Puzzle

Across	Down
3. [ɔfʊl]	1. [θɔŋ]
5. [lɑŋ]	2. [fʊt]
6. [to]	4. [lo]
7. [sok]	5. [lus]

Back Vowel Transcription Exercise 12–11
AUDIO 2–37

1. ['kupɑn]   11. ['kʊkbʊk]
2. [hʊk]   12. ['bostfʊl]
3. ['ɑnkor]   13. ['fʊtstul]
4. [hɑ'θorn]   14. ['horsʃu]
5. ['nuzrum]   15. [fɔt]
6. ['tɑko]   16. ['dormrum]
7. ['jojo]   17. [frut]
8. ['ɔfʊl]   18. ['mɑθbɔl]
9. [jɑt]   19. [sok]
10. [lɑlipɑp]   20. ['θɔtfʊl]

Chapter 13

/aɪ/ I-M-F Table Transcription Exercise 13–1
AUDIO 2–38

1. [aɪlɪnd]   I
2. [aɪ]   I
3. [gaɪ]   F
4. [maɪnəs]   M
5. [daɪl]   M
6. [raɪm]   M
7. [swit]
8. [haɪ]   F
9. [nis]
10. [braɪd]   M

/aɪ/ Transcription Exercise 13–2
AUDIO 2–39

1. [baɪ]
2. ['saɪdɚ]
3. [haɪt]
4. ['faɪsti]
5. [slaɪs]
6. [taɪm]
7. [raɪt]
8. [saɪ]
9. [raɪm]

/aʊ/ I-M-F Table Transcription Exercise 13–3
AUDIO 2–40

1. [aʊtʃ]   I
2. [lɑn]
3. [kaʊwɚd]   M
4. [vaʊwəl]   M
5. [haʊ]   F
6. [tɑfi]
7. [ʃaʊt]   M
8. [no]
9. [laʊndʒ]   M
10. [haʊs]   M

/aʊ/ Transcription Exercise 13–4
AUDIO 2–41

1. [aʊst]
2. [traʊt]
3. ['gaʊdʒɪŋ]
4. [praʊwəl]
5. ['tʃaʊdɚ]
6. ['haʊshold]
7. [baʊnd]
8. [laʊs]
9. [baʊ]

/ɔɪ/ I-M-F Table Transcription Exercise 13–5
AUDIO 2–42

1. [kɔɪ]   F
2. [tʃɔɪs]   M
3. [taʊn]
4. [dʒɔɪn]   M
5. [saɪfɚ]
6. [mɔɪst]   M
7. [mɪst]
8. [bɔɪjɛnt]   M
9. [dʒus]
10. [spɔɪl]   M

/ɔɪ/ Transcription Exercise 13–6
AUDIO 2–43

1. ['hɔɪstɪŋ]
2. ['kɔɪld]
3. ['dɛstrɔɪ]
4. [fɔɪlz]
5. ['lɔɪtɚ]
6. ['vɔɪsɪŋ]
7. [tɔɪ]
8. [ɛks'plɔɪt]
9. [ə'vɔɪd]

/ju/ I-M-F Table Transcription Exercise 13–7
AUDIO 2–44

1. [fju]   F
2. [junjən]   I
3. [bjuti]   M
4. [kjut]   M
5. [pju]   F
6. [juz]   I
7. [hjudʒ]   M
8. [ful]
9. [hjumɚ]   M
10. [hulə]

/ju/ Transcription Exercise 13–8
AUDIO 2–45

1. [juk]
2. ['fjuʃə]
3. ['mjuzɪk]
4. [hjudʒ]
5. ['mjutɪnt]
6. ['pjupəl]
7. [spjud]
8. [bjut]
9. [fjum]

Diphthong Crossword Puzzle

Across	Down
1. [mɔɪst]	1. [mju]
3. [kju]	2. [spɔɪld]
4. [daʊn]	5. [naʊn]
6. [naɪn]	7. [aɪsaɪt]

Diphthong Transcription Exercise 13–9
AUDIO 2–46

1. ['faʊndri]
2. [dʒɔɪn]
3. ['jukɑn]
4. [braɪn]
5. [tɔɪl]
6. [dʒænjuwɛri]
7. [aʊst]
8. ['jukəleli]
9. [mɔɪst]
10. ['æmjulɛt]
11. [paʊt]
12. [baɪt]
13. [naʊn]
14. [nɔɪz]
15. ['fraʊnɪŋ]
16. [aɪ]
17. [kʌntrɪbjutɚ]
18. [ɔɪŋk]
19. [maɪm]
20. ['braʊniz]

Chapter 14

Transcription Exercise 14–2 (#6–10)
AUDIO 2–48

Stressed syllable is in **bold** print.

Noun	Verb
6. 'record	6. re'**cord**
7. 'invalid	7. in'**valid**
8. 'desert	8. de'**sert**
9. 'refuse	9. re'**fuse**
10. 'present	10. pre'**sent**

Transcription Exercise 14–3
AUDIO 2–49

	Syllable Division	Number of Syllables
1. 'licorice	lic-or-ice	(3)
2. in'gredient	in-gre-di-ent	(4)
3. 'crying	cry-ing	(2)
4. a'nother	a-noth-er	(3)
5. 'audible	au-di-ble	(3)
6. hi'larious	hi-lar-i-ous	(4)
7. se'curity	se-cu-ri-ty	(4)
8. com'puter	com-put-er	(3)
9. 'saxophone	sax-o-phone	(3)
10. 'bigger	big-ger	(2)
11. 'pleasure	plea-sure	(2)
12. aggra'vation	ag-gra-va-tion	(4)
13. 'aftermath	af-ter-math	(3)
14. 'resource	re-source	(2)
15. pre'pare	pre-pare	(2)
16. 'liberal	lib-er-al	(3)
17. water'melon	wa-ter-mel-on	(4)
18. gener'ation	gen-er-a-tion	(4)
19. e'vaporate	e-vap-o-rate	(4)
20. 'public	pub-lic	(2)

Chapter 15

Transcription Exercise 15–1
AUDIO 2–50

1. [fɪkst]	11. ['fregræn's]
2. ['kæn'səl]	12. ['stʌmɪks]
3. [stɑp:ʊʃɪŋ]	13. [kɪsɚ]
4. [dʒʌɪŋk]	14. ['kʌmpfɚt]
5. [pʊʃt]	15. [blæk:orn]
6. [drɛmpt]	16. [bʌgz]
7. [go'we]	17. [lɛmigo]
8. [wɪgz]	18. [prɪn's]
9. [mɪŋk]	19. [sidz]
10. [lɪtəl:usi]	20. [θɪn:aɪf]

Chapter 4 Word Search #1: /p/ and /b/

Chapter 4 Word Search #2:
/t/, /d/, /k/, and /g/

Chapter 5 Word Search #3: /m/ and /n/

m	e	m	æ	g	n	o	l	j	ə	l	n
d	o	ə	p	k	d	ɚ	i	e	ɪ	z	ɛ
ɛ	f	o	r	dʒ	u	ʌ	p	ɛ	u	ŋ	r
l	r	ð	ɪ	n	n	s	i	ɪ	o	p	v
f	s	m	m	ʌ	m	t	t	u	o	æ	θ
ɪ	p	ʃ	r	j	v	ks	u	ʊ	ɚ	n	g
n	b	t	o	d	f	k	n	b	ɚ	z	o
i	t	ɪ	z	e	p	ɑ	i	i	ə	i	k
ə	d	s	o	m	ɛ	r	ə	g	o	l	d
m	k	r	p	i	o	n	i	o	ʌ	s	h
ə	g	ʊ	z	tʃ	w	e	ʒ	n	k	s	ʒ
dʒ	æ	z	m	i	n	ʃ	z	i	g	z	z
j	w	ɔ	ɪ	æ	n	ə	e	ə	s	r	v
ʌ	z	ɪ	n	i	ə	n	w	o	z	w	f

Chapter 6 Word Search #5: /f/ and /v/

v	ɪ	k	t	ɔ	r	i	h	e	d	ɪ	n
m	h	ɛ	g	d	e	t	r	r	b	s	h
ɑ	r	r	ɪ	t	ɚ	m	ɛ	n	k	ɛ
r	ɛ	ə	v	ɪ	n	s	k	s	ɑ	k	p
s	f	ʊ	t	b	ɔ	l	i	i	l	ɪ	d
u	ɚ	n	d	h	ɑ	r	v	v	i	k	ə
n	i	ə	s	e	f	t	i	ɚ	t	c	h
b	l	u	d	w	ɪ	i	v	g	u	f	æ
f	ʊ	l	b	æ	k	l	ɑ	m	p	r	f
r	w	f	ɑ	d	s	w	r	θ	ɛ	e	b
ʊ	u	i	dʒ	d	ə	ʃ	s	ɛ	r	n	æ
k	d	l	u	æ	m	æ	ɪ	r	i	i	k
s	b	d	l	i	t	m	t	i	dʒ	ɛ	r
ɔ	f	ɛ	n	s	a	d	i	f	ɛ	n	s

Chapter 5 Word Search #4: /ŋ/

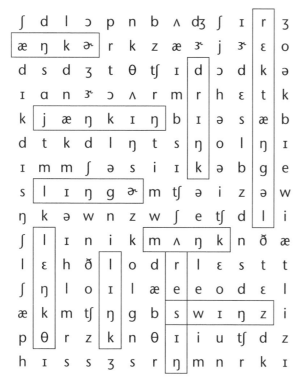

Chapter 6 Word Search #6: /s/ and /z/

æ	h	m	s	t	o	a	g	ɪ	t	m	k
k	æ	ɛ	l	ə	f	ɪ	n	t	s	z	a
r	m	t	i	ɚ	r	h	d	r	k	ɛ	s
o	h	p	s	ɛ	ks	aɪ	t	m	ɛ	n	t
b	u	ɛ	ə	m	i	d	r	ɛ	o	tʃ	u
æ	t	r	m	ɛ	ə	h	æ	k	r	ə	m
t	b	i	s	m	l	aʊ	p	i	n	i	z
s	ɚ	k	ə	s	d	r	i	t	p	a	l
j	ɑ	h	ɪ	k	e	g	z	i	b	r	ə
h	ð	æ	r	l	l	e	e	u	o	k	ɑ
u	k	l	k	aʊ	e	t	aɪ	g	ɚ	z	r
p	æ	o	n	n	b	d	dʒ	d	t	o	z
s	t	w	l	z	n	ɔ	ɚ	i	e	t	i
s	l	aɪ	ə	n	z	r	t	ɛ	n	t	s

Chapter 6 Word Search #7: /θ/ and /ð/

```
g t k ɛ l v b ʌ k b m s
ɝ ʒ p æ θ h e b m ɛ θ aʊ
k p o r ɛ e ð ɛ ɪ d ð d
l p θ t m v m ɛ o e æ m
o o r æ ð b ɑ ð ɚ l n ɑ
ð k ɛ n p f θ l d t t m
e θ d d ə n ə ð ɚ p æ æ
v n k m g tʃ æ t ə k n θ
æ ɚ ð g r θ ɪ ŋ l l r ɪ
θ n t æ ɚ ɚ θ ɚ z ɑ t ɛ
r g n ð v d r w ɪ θ aʊ t
j b o ɚ k h ɪ b s e t i
ə æ g m s aʊ θ ɑ l m ɛ g
t θ t θ p z n r i æ n k
```

Chapter 7 Word Search #9: /tʃ/ and /dʒ/

```
k p a s s a g e z e dʒ i p b r j m ɛ
n k w tʃ k v u i tʃ ʍ o f z g j r s n
d b t s i ə b ɛ ks tʃ e n dʒ n u tʃ v d
j s p k æ z h v s t o h i g m v ɪ z
m j æ h u h a h w n ɛ w f dʒ p r l t
p æ d v ɛ n tʃ ɚ k θ u p ʌ z s p ɪ m
m e o z v l ɝ p æ s ɪ dʒ ɛ p o k dʒ n
m m s h p b f o g s t ʃ dʒ h w g g ŋ
g a dʒ ɪ ŋ k s s t z æ l ɪ o e æ ʌ ɑ
t v ɪ f k g θ c ɔ ʃ l k ʊ j h s u ʍ
v d l i æ o n d dʒ h l m f v ʌ s ə j
t f ɛ r ʌ i ʒ r n ʒ f æ æ z f n s r
r b r ɪ dʒ ɛ z l ɪ m z dʒ p ɛ ɪ b z l
j b w e ɪ f ŋ ɪ l n m ɪ v ks h i ʃ ʌ
i w o o k v ɛ ʊ æ ŋ d k m u w tʃ h ɛ
l n h r ʃ ð n ɚ tʃ ɔ o v h n j p ʒ p
ʊ z s ɪ n tʃ ə p f o s p ɛ h t i tʃ t
z h t u t h ʍ b v u n ʒ l m r w dʒ d
```

Chapter 6 Word Search #8: /ʃ/ and /ʒ/

```
ʃ æ l o k ʃ s z n æ aɪ p
d d d p r r ɪ ɪ k n g ɔ
ɪ l ʌ æ o ɪ t k θ o l l
k n k n j m i l ɪ ʃ k ə
d r m ʃ ɪ p s s ŋ ə r n
ɪ ɑ ə d u r m l s n ɑ i
s d ɪ s n o ə z z d f ʒ
n s n d t f ɪ ʃ k r ɚ ə
ʃ o l e θ e ð ɔ o u j k
i m m l w z ʃ ə l ʃ æ d
ʃ ɑ r k d i l ə h w b o
l i s p r o n ð n ɛ r l
æ t r ɛ ʒ ɚ tʃ ɛ s t t æ
p m k l æ m ʃ ɛ l b m b
h ɪ tʃ u o d ɔ ə s ɚ ɪ ʒ
d k ɪ z b ʌ r l ɛ m n r
```

Chapter 8 Word Search #10: /w/

```
g w a n t a n a m o b e
ʃ ɛ w e r s ð r d b ʃ s
s a b s ð ŋ l r j o m h
æ p v ɪ v o ʃ tʃ b m n aʊ
n a k v f w a t ɚ l u w
w p r ɪ i ʌ ə j v w θ ɪ
a w ɚ l d w ɔ r w ʌ n t
n tʃ ɪ w p b t d k g s z
h a b ɔ r æ p e p k w ɚ
ɪ ʒ r e dʒ ɚ u o θ
l ʃ æ ʊ t b n z b l ɑ ð
r w ɛ p ə n e w l d j ɝ
d p ɛ t e v i h b w e m
p æ n d p aʊ w ɚ ʊ c l u
ɚ z d ɔ l t r d ʒ r v i
```

Chapter 8 Word Search #11: Vowel + r

Chapter 10 Word Search #13: Front Vowels

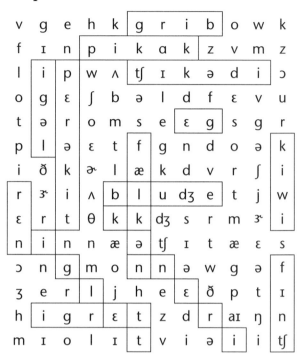

Chapter 8 Word Search #12: /j/, /l/, and /r/

Chapter 11 Word Search #14: /ɚ/ and /ɝ/

Chapter 12 Word Search #15: Back Vowels

```
s ʃ r ɑ dʒ ɚ d ɔ l t r i z v m f ʍ
dʒ ʒ ɚ k j u ə b ɑ ɑ z ð ʌ ɝ ɑ n ɪ
b ʌ dʒ ɔ z j o r ɑ r i r ɛ v æ ʌ k
ʊ k p s θ i s ɑ ɛ t æ ɪ w m n u d
l r ɛ k h n dʒ b ʊ g s z ð e d o r
w ʌ p z s u z ɪ n l u tʃ i w p m ɔ
ɪ p v t ð i z n z ɪ l o p h ɑ d m
ŋ æ k s ʃ u k ʍ h f n v ɛ o b k f ɑ
k s g t o θ p ʊ m p ʒ o p s ɛ ɪ g
l ɪ u æ l j h d ʊ g ŋ m n p t l r
b w f e w o k ʍ tʃ ɪ o u e i l z ɔ
h a i ə ʌ g ɑ r θ b r ʊ k s o g s
n k w tʃ æ z ʌ z h t w b v u n ʒ d
s ʍ ɪ k d r ɔ m ə g r ɔ j h i g t
j r u p ɔ l ɚ f ɛ ɝ b f dʒ u w e l
l ks ɪ dʒ o r dʒ b ʊ ʃ t s f z r s n
```

Chapter 13 Word Search #16: Diphthongs

```
s ʃ r d o n p ɚ r ɔ t t v
h aɪ æ k s v ju z p n ə v ʌ
d s t ə ɛ c ɛ b ɔɪ n r d
b h i n b w w r b s z f k
s aʊ ɛ t k z ʌ u ʊ t i h p
h s aʊ θ b aʊ n d m ɚ b ju s
f p ʒ m ɪ g z i m ʒ u m n
k æ w aɪ l d f aʊ l æ ʊ ɚ p
l ɛ t n æ k h ʌ ɪ k s n æ
b b s θ p ə r z d p i g s
h ɪ f ŋ s ɔɪ l v z ɔɪ v ʒ z
n ju æ l ks dʒ t ʃ e z i z f
s b z f ju ʃ ə t r w g ɔ aɪ
o ɪ k aʊ tʃ g j r æ m ɑ ɚ j
```

C

Answers to Study Questions

Chapter 1

1. To accurately transcribe the speech of a client and so that another professional can identify how speech sounds were produced.

2. Greek.

3. A sound/symbol system used to represent the sounds of all languages.

4. Must learn a new sound/symbol system for the majority of the IPA vowels.

5. Study of speech sounds.

6. a. Organs that produce speech and their function (physiological phonetics)
   b. Physical properties of speech sounds (acoustic phonetics)
   c. Process of speech sound perception (perceptual phonetics)

7. a. /ʃ/
   b. /θ/ /ð/
   c. /ŋ/
   d. /i/
   e. /ə/
   f. /æ/

8. Phonemic (broad transcription) does not use diacritic marks to specify how a speech sound was produced (narrow transcription).

Chapter 2

1. "C"—Consonant
   "V"—Vowel

2. Initial: First sound heard
   Medial: Sound in middle of a word
   Final: Last sound heard at end of the word

3. Prevocalic: Consonant preceding a vowel
   Intervocalic: Consonant occurring between two vowels
   Postvocalic: Consonant after a vowel

4. Nucleus: Vowel of a syllable
   Onset: Consonant that releases the nucleus of a syllable
   Coda: Consonant after a vowel

5. A vowel, diphthong, or syllabic consonant

6. Open syllable: "bee"
   Closed syllable: "beet"

7. "scrape"
   C C C V C
   s k r e p

8. How a word is spelled

Chapter 3

1. Survival function

2. Phonation Articulation Respiration Resonation

3. Place: *Where* the speech sound is produced
   Manner: *How* the speech sound is produced

4. In the nasal cavity

5. Adducted: Vocal folds *close* and vibrate
   Abducted: Vocal folds *open* and do not vibrate

6. a. lips
   b. glottis
   c. tongue and upper and lower teeth
   d. alveolar ridge
   e. hard palate
   f. velum or soft palate

7. Two or three consonants in the same syllable

8. Obstruent: Obstruction of vocal tract
   Sonorant: Open channel not blocked

Chapter 4

1. Air is stopped in oral cavity; air is released.

2. Vocal folds adduct to hold air in glottis; vocal folds abduct to open and release air.

3. Only voicing differs.

4. Tongue tip and blade briefly contact, or flaps, against upper Alveolar ridge.

5. Glottal stop/voiced /t/ and alveolar flap

6. a. /g/
   b. /d/
   c. /b/

7. a. Allophonic variation of /t/ and /k/
   b. NOT written as a question mark
   c. When glottal stop is followed by /n/, a syllabic /n̩/ is used.

Chapter 5

1. /m/n/ŋ/

2. /m/ is a bilabial (produced with both lips), /n/ is a lingua-alveolar, /ŋ/ is a lingua-velar.

3. Made in the *same place* as another phoneme

4. A consonant that acts like a vowel

5. Formal: Used in a formal setting, such as giving a speech
Casual: Speaking with friends or family

6. Homorganic relationships: /n/t,d,s,z /m/b,p /ŋ/k,g

7. A (̩) is placed below the syllabic consonant, for example, /m̩/.

Chapter 6

1. Both phonemes are unvoiced when produced in isolation.

2. Glottis

3. Tongue position not relevant

4. Tongue tip up: At upper alveolar ridge behind central incisors
Tongue tip down: Contacts lower incisors behind lower alveolar ridge

5. Interdental: Breath stream emitted between central incisors
Lateral: Breath stream emitted around the sides of the tongue

6. Theta

7. Sides contact upper molars; tip at lower central incisors; front of tongue elevates toward hard palate

Chapter 7

1. /t/ and /ʃ/ for /tʃ/ /d/ and /ʒ/ for /dʒ/

2. Stop-fricatives

3. Produced with an obstructed breath stream

4. /t/d/ or omitted

5. /tʃ/   a. children   b. ketchup
/dʒ/   a. region   b. joke

6. To eliminate confusing the symbols as two separate phonemes

Chapter 8

1. Approximation of the articulators

2. It can occur between a word ending in /i/ adjacent to a word beginning with /ɪ/ when the words are spoken as one utterance, for example, "she is" [ʃijɪz].

3. /kw/ or /kʍ/

4. Lateral airflow around the sides of the tongue

5. a. Robert
b. carrot
c. fairy
d. sparkle
e. portrait

6. Position of closeness of articulators which causes some constriction

Chapter 9

1. A syllable must contain a vowel or diphthong.

2. Tongue does not make contact with a specific articulator for closure

3. The vocal tract is mostly unobstructed.

4. Monophthong: Single sound (one vowel)
Diphthong: Two sounds (two vowels)

5. Provides reference for tongue position

6. Vertical: Height of tongue
Horizontal: Tongue advancement

7. A tense tongue requires muscular tension at root of tongue; a lax tongue requires less muscular tension at root of tongue.

Chapter 10

1. Unrounded, slightly retracted

2. Short "i."

3. /æ/ also called "ash"

4. squid myth built

5. /æ/

6. /ɛ/

7. /eɪ/

Chapter 11

1. /ɚ/ /ɝ/

2. Middle of the oral cavity

3. a. /ɝ/ produced with greater duration
   b. /ɝ/ can form a syllable
   c. tongue moves toward the /r/ consonant
   d. /r/ is voiceless following a voiceless consonant

4. The midcentral lax vowel (unrounded/unstressed).

5. "Duh!"

6. /ɚ/

7. Stressed syllables

Chapter 12

1. /ɑ/

2. Lips round or slightly protrude

3. Upsilon

4. /ʊ/u/o/

5. bushel crook wolves put

Chapter 13

1. Two vowels spoken in sequence (in continuation)

2. There is a gradual movement of the articulators from one vowel to another

3. ‿ To indicate two vowel sounds in each diphthongs are used together

4. /aɪ/ /aʊ/ /ɔɪ/

5. /ju͡/

6. /aɪ͡/

Chapter 14

1. Accent

2. Most prominent part of a syllable in a multisyllabic word or word in a phrase

3. Stress is placed on first or second syllable. For example: **sus**pect (noun: someone *suspected* of something) and sus**pect** (verb: believe someone is *guilty* of something)

4. Majority of morphological markers do not change stress in a word. The stress is usually on the root word and first syllable of a two-syllable word.

5. Words of two syllables have the same amount of stress, for example, textbook.

6. Stress has been associated with: (a) high amplitude (loudness), (b) long duration of the syllable nucleus (time), and (c) high frequency (pitch) of the syllable nucleus.

Chapter 15

1. Adjustment or adaptation of speech sounds due to phonetic environment

2. Phonemes that surround a specific speech sound

3. Assimilation and coarticulation.

4. Progressive: Occurs left to right; a *preceding* phoneme influences the phoneme. Regressive: Occurs right to left; a phoneme is changed by one that *follows* it.

5. It occurs as a result of the rapid rate of speech. It produces minor phonetic changes.

6. A symbol to indicate a specific way a phoneme was produced

7. Lengthening diacritic is ː or ˑ

8. It is when a voiced phoneme is adjacent to an unvoiced phoneme, for example, price [praɪs̥].

9. Elision: A phoneme is omitted in a word, for example, "cam-er-a" [kæmrə]. Epenthesis: A phoneme can be added, for example, "spoon" [səpun].

Chapter 16

1. Accent-free speech.

2. A variation of speech or language

3. Speech characteristics of a foreign dialect

4. East, Midwest, and Southern states

5. /t/ substitution for /θ/ in Initial position; consonant cluster reduction; /r/ phoneme lessened or omitted

6. b/v substitution, schwa inserted before Initial consonant clusters, Spanish "s" produced frontally

Listening Activities

Stop-Consonants /p/b/t/d/k/g/

Listening Activity 1
AUDIO 3–1

Initial position /p/b/

/p/	/b/
1. pill	bill
2. peas	bees
3. pack	back
4. pet	bet
5. patch	batch
6. pat	bat

Final position /p/b/

/p/	/b/
1. cap	cab
2. rope	robe
3. rip	rub
4. pop	rob
5. lap	lab
6. ape	Abe

Listening Activity 2
AUDIO 3–2

Initial position /t/d/

/t/	/d/
1. ton	done
2. tame	dame
3. tie	die
4. toe	doe
5. tea	Dee
6. try	dry

Final position /t/d/

/t/	/d/
1. molt	mold
2. cat	cad
3. fate	fade
4. sat	sad
5. boat	bode
6. at	add

Listening Activity 3
AUDIO 3–3

Initial position /k/g/

/k/	/g/
1. come	gum
2. cut	gut
3. curl	girl
4. cap	gap
5. came	game
6. could	good

Final position /k/g/

/k/	/g/
1. tack	tag
2. pluck	plug
3. back	bag
4. rack	rag
5. shack	shag
6. luck	lug

Nasals /m/n/ŋ/

Note. /ŋ/ is not found in Initial position in Standard American English.

Listening Activity 4
AUDIO 3–4

Initial position /m/n/

/m/	/n/
1. moat	note
2. mail	nail
3. met	net
4. mow	no
5. mob	knob
6. map	nap

Final position /m/n/

/m/	/n/
1. sum	sun
2. home	hone
3. ram	ran
4. rum	run
5. tam	tan
6. beam	bean

Final position /m/ŋ/

/m/	/ŋ/
1. swim	swing
2. Kim	king
3. ream	ring
4. bomb	wrong
5. Sam	sang
6. hum	hung

Final Position /n/ŋ/

/n/	/ŋ/
1. thin	thing
2. win	wing
3. pin	ping
4. sun	sung
5. ran	rang
6. kin	king

Fricatives /s/z/f/v/ʃ/ʒ/θ/ð/h/hw/

Listening Activity 5
AUDIO 3–5

Initial position /s/z/

/s/	/z/
1. sip	zip
2. sack	Zach
3. sue	zoo
4. sag	zag
5. sap	zap
6. seal	zeal

Final position /s/z/

/s/	/z/
1. bus	buzz
2. mace	maze
3. loose	lose
4. race	raise
5. peace	peas
6. price	prize

Listening Activity 6
AUDIO 3–6

Initial position /f/v/

/f/	/v/
1. fan	van
2. fault	vault
3. fail	veil
4. fine	vine
5. file	vile
6. feign	vein

Final position /f/v/

/f/	/v/
1. leaf	leave
2. sheaf	sheave
3. proof	prove
4. waif	wave
5. safe	save
6. strife	strive

Listening Activity 7
AUDIO 3–7

Note. The /ʒ/ phoneme does not appear in the Initial position and is not used frequently in the Final word position in Standard American English. The contrasts are presented in Medial position of words.

Medial position /ʃ/ʒ/

/ʃ/	/ʒ/
1. vicious	vision
2. pressure	pleasure
3. dilution	delusion
4. assure	azure
5. glacier	glazier
6. vacation	occasion

Listening Activity 8
AUDIO 3–8

Note. This activity also includes the /d/ substitution for /ð/. This substitution occurs frequently in children.

All positions /θ/ð/

/θ/	/ð/
1. breath	breathe
2. wreath	wreathe
3. bath	bathe
4. thigh	thy
5. ether	either
6. cloth	clothe

All positions /d/ð/

/d/	/ð/
1. reed	wreathe
2. den	then
3. fodder	father
4. day	they
5. doze	those
6. dough	though

Listening Activity 9
AUDIO 3–9

Note. /h/ does not appear in Final word position in Standard American English.

Initial position /h/

/h/	omission of /h/
1. had	add
2. heat	eat
3. hair	air
4. hoops	oops
5. hit	it
6. hate	ate

Listening Activity 10
AUDIO 3–10

Note. /hw/ or /ʍ/ does not appear in the Final word position in Standard American English, and is often produced as /w/ in the Initial and Medial word positions.

Initial position /h/hw/

/h/	/hw/
1. hut	what
2. heel	wheel
3. heat	wheat
4. hen	when
5. him	whim
6. hail	whale

Affricates /tʃ/dʒ/

Listening Activity 11
AUDIO 3–11

Initial position /tʃ/dʒ/

/tʃ/	/dʒ/
1. chunk	junk
2. chug	jug
3. cheap	jeep
4. choke	joke
5. chin	gin
6. chain	Jane

Final position /tʃ/dʒ/

/tʃ/	/dʒ/
1. match	Madge
2. lunch	lunge
3. rich	ridge
4. etch	edge
5. scrunch	grunge
6. batch	badge

Listening Activity 12
AUDIO 3–12

Second language learners often confuse /tʃ/ for /ʃ/. Here are some contrast words:

/tʃ/	/ʃ/
1. cheek	chic
2. ditch	dish
3. chip	ship
4. watched	washed
5. march	marsh
6. batch	bash

Oral Resonants /w/j/l/r/

Listening Activity 13
AUDIO 3–13

All positions /r/l/

/r/	/l/
1. rare	lair
2. crowd	cloud
3. near	kneel
4. reap	leap
5. pray	play
6. rate	late

Listening Activity 14
AUDIO 3–14

Initial position /j/w/

/j/	/w/
1. yell	well
2. Yale	wail
3. yield	wield
4. yaks	wax
5. yoke	woke
6. yes	Wes

Listening Activity 15
AUDIO 3–15

Note. The phoneme /j/ is often confused with /dʒ/, especially with students learning English as a second language. The following listening activity contrasts these phonemes.

Initial position /dʒ/j/

/dʒ/	/j/
1. Jack	yak
2. joke	yoke
3. jam	yam
4. Jell-O	yellow
5. jail	Yale
6. jet	yet

Front Vowels /i/ɪ/e/ɛ/æ/

Note. Because not all vowels are found in the Initial and the Final positions of words, the Medial position has been included.

Listening Activity 16
AUDIO 3–16

Note. The Final position for these vowels is not included, as there is discussion regarding whether /i/ or /ɪ/ occurs in Final word position. See Singh and Singh (2006) for a discussion. Initial and Medial position /i/ɪ/

	/i/	/ɪ/
1.	eat	it
2.	beat	bit
3.	deep	dip
4.	eel	ill
5.	peak	pick
6.	peach	pitch

Listening Activity 17
AUDIO 3–17

Medial position /i/e/

	/i/	/e/
1.	grease	Grace
2.	reed	raid
3.	team	tame
4.	weed	wade
5.	treat	trait
6.	green	grain

Listening Activity 18
AUDIO 3–18

Medial position /i/ɛ/

	/i/	/ɛ/
1.	teen	ten
2.	bead	bed
3.	keep	kept
4.	seat	set
5.	meat	met
6.	we'll	well

Listening Activity 19
AUDIO 3–19

Medial position /ɪ/e/

	/ɪ/	/e/
1.	lit	late
2.	tip	tape
3.	chin	chain
4.	grid	grade
5.	tick	take
6.	till	tale

Listening Activity 20
AUDIO 3–20

Medial position /ɪ/ɛ/

	/ɪ/	/ɛ/
1.	bid	bed
2.	will	well
3.	hid	head
4.	tin	ten
5.	mitt	met
6.	knit	net

Listening Activity 21
AUDIO 3–21

Medial position /e/ɛ/

	/e/	/ɛ/
1.	laid	led
2.	date	debt
3.	main	men
4.	mate	met
5.	bait	bet
6.	fade	fed

Listening Activity 22
AUDIO 3–22

Medial position /æ/ɛ/

	/æ/	/ɛ/
1.	bat	bet
2.	had	head
3.	lad	led
4.	gnat	net
5.	sat	set
6.	sand	send

Central Vowels /ə/ʌ/ɚ/ɝ/

Note. As discussed in Chapter 11, the stressed and unstressed central vowels sound very similar. To provide a contrast, the /ɝ/ and /ʌ/ are presented in words.

Listening Activity 23
AUDIO 3–23

Medial position /ɝ/ʌ/

	/ɝ/	/ʌ/
1.	curt	cut
2.	shirk	shuck
3.	hurt	hut
4.	shirt	shut
5.	burn	bun
6.	lurk	luck

Listening Activity 24
AUDIO 3–24

/ɝ/ contrast with vowel + /r/

/ɝ/	ir	ɑr	or	ɛr
1. burr	beer	bar	bore	bear
2. fur	fear	far	for	fair
3. spur	spear	spar	spore	spare
4. stir	steer	star	store	stare
5. purr	peer	par	pore	pear
6. bird	beard	bard	bored	bared

Back Vowels /u/ʊ/o/ɔ/ɑ/

Listening Activity 25
AUDIO 3–25

Medial position /u/ʊ/

/u/	/ʊ/
1. Luke	look
2. fool	full
3. kook	cook
4. pool	pull
5. cooed	could
6. stewed	stood

Listening Activity 26
AUDIO 3–26

Medial position /o/ʊ/

/o/	/ʊ/
1. goad	good
2. coke	cook
3. pole	pull
4. stowed	stood
5. bowl	bull
6. broke	brook

Listening Activity 27
AUDIO 3–27

Medial position /o/ /ɑ/ or /ɔ/ depending on dialect

/o/	/ɑ/ or /ɔ/
1. load	laud
2. coat	caught
3. loan	lawn
4. boat	bought
5. sewed	sawed
6. bowl	bawl

Listening Activity 28
AUDIO 3–28

/ɑ/ and /ɔ/ depending on dialect

/ɑ/	/ɔ/
1. Otto	auto
2. not	naught
3. rot	wrought
4. pod	pawed
5. tot	taught
6. cot	caught

Back vowel contrast with /ʌ/

Listening Activity 29
AUDIO 3–29

Medial position /ʌ/u/

/ʌ/	/u/
1. dumb	doom
2. done	dune
3. rum	room
4. nut	newt
5. sun	soon
6. spun	spoon

Listening Activity 30
AUDIO 3–30

Medial position /ʌ/ʊ/

/ʌ/	/ʊ/
1. putt	put
2. tuck	took
3. luck	look
4. cud	could
5. stud	stood
6. shuck	shook

Listening Activity 31
AUDIO 3–31

Medial position /ʌ/ɑ/ and /ɔ/ depending on dialect

/ʌ/	/ɑ/ or /ɔ/
1. duck	dock
2. bum	bomb
3. come	calm
4. cut	cot
5. sum	psalm
6. nut	not

Diphthongs /aɪ/aʊ/ɔɪ/ju/

Listening Activity 32
AUDIO 3–32

Medial and Final position /aɪ/aʊ/

/aɪ/	/aʊ/
1. high	how
2. spite	spout
3. mice	mouse
4. by	bow
5. file	fowl
6. nine	noun

Listening Activity 33
AUDIO 3–33

Medial and Final position /aɪ/ɔɪ/

/aɪ/	/ɔɪ/
1. pies	poise
2. file	foil
3. tile	toil
4. vice	voice
5. buy	boy
6. ties	toys

Listening Activity 34
AUDIO 3–34

Medial and Final position /ju/aɪ/

/ju/	/aɪ/
1. hue	high
2. butte	bite
3. mute	might
4. cute	kite
5. mew	my
6. pew	pie

Table of Contents for Audio Files

CD 1 – Transcription Exercises

CD 2 – Transcription Exercises

CD 3 – Listening Activities

CD 4 – Phoneme Study Cards

Audio	Study Card	Phoneme	Audio	Study Card	Phoneme
4–1	SC 1	/k/	4–25	SC 25	/w/
4–2	SC 2	/g/	4–26	SC 26	/i/
4–3	SC 3	/p/	4–27	SC 27	/ɪ/
4–4	SC 4	/b/	4–28	SC 28	/ɛ/
4–5	SC 5	/t/	4–29	SC 29	/e/
4–6	SC 6	/d/	4–30	SC 30	/æ/
4–7	SC 7	/s/	4–31	SC 31	/ə/
4–8	SC 8	/z/	4–32	SC 32	/ʌ/
4–9	SC 9	/f/	4–33	SC 33	/ɚ/
4–10	SC 10	/v/	4–34	SC 34	/ɝ/
4–11	SC 11	/θ/	4–35	SC 35	/u/
4–12	SC 12	/ð/	4–36	SC 36	/ʊ/
4–13	SC 13	/ʃ/	4–37	SC 37	/o/
4–14	SC 14	/ʒ/	4–38	SC 38	/ɔ/
4–15	SC 15	/h/	4–39	SC 39	/ɑ/
4–16	SC 16	/hw/	4–40	SC 40	/aɪ/
4–17	SC 17	/tʃ/	4–41	SC 41	/aʊ/
4–18	SC 18	/dʒ/	4–42	SC 42	/ɔɪ/
4–19	SC 19	/m/	4–43	SC 43	/ju/
4–20	SC 20	/n/	4–44	SC 44	/ɑr/
4–21	SC 21	/ŋ/	4–45	SC 45	/or/
4–22	SC 22	/l/	4–46	SC 46	/ir/
4–23	SC 23	/j/	4–47	SC 47	/ɛr/
4–24	SC 24	/r/			

References

Arlt, P. B., & Goodban, M. T. (1976) A comparative study of articulation acquisition as based on a study of 240 normals, aged three to six. *Language, Speech and Hearing Services in Schools, 7,* 173–180.

Battle, D. E. (Ed.). (2012). *Communicative disorders in multicultural and international populations* (4th ed.). St Louis, MO: Elsevier.

Bernthal, J., & Bankson, N. (1998). Phonological assessment procedures. In *Articulation and phonological disorders* (4th ed.). Boston, MA: Allyn & Bacon.

Edwards, H. T. (2003). *Applied phonetics: The sounds of American English* (3rd ed.). Clifton Park, NY: Thomson Delmar Learning.

Fudala, J. B., & Reynolds, W. M. (1986) *Arizona Articulation Proficiency Scale* (2nd ed.) Austin, TX: Pro-Ed.

Garn-Nunn, P., & Lynn, J. (2004). *Calvert's descriptive phonetics* (3rd ed.). New York, NY: Thieme.

Hegde, M. N., & Pomaville, F. (2013). *Assessment of communicative disorders in children* (2nd ed.). San Diego, CA: Plural.

Ladefoged, P. (2005). *Vowels and consonants* (2nd ed.). Malden, MA: Blackwell.

Lowe, R. J., & Blosser, J. (2002). *Workbook for identification of phonological processes and distinctive features* (4th ed.). Austin, TX: Pro-Ed.

MacKay, I. (1987). *Phonetics: The science of speech production* (2nd ed.) Boston, MA: Allyn & Bacon.

Mann, W. (2012). *Hello, gorgeous: Becoming Barbra Streisand.* Boston, MA: Houghton Mifflin Harcourt.

McLaughlin, S. (2006). *Introduction to language development* (2nd ed.) Clifton Park, NY: Thomson Delmar Learning.

Pena-Brooks, A., & Hegde, M. N. (2007). *Assessment and treatment of phonological disorders in children.* Austin, TX: Pro-Ed.

Poole, I. (1934). Genetic development of consonant sounds in English. *Elementary English Review, 11,* 159–161.

Prather, E. M., Hedrick, E. L., & Kerin, C. A. (1975). Articulation development in children aged two to four years. *Journal of Speech and Hearing Disorders, 40,* 179–191.

Roseberry-McKibbin, C. (2014). *Multicultural students with special needs: Practical strategies for assessment and intervention* (4th ed.). Oceanside, CA: Academic Communication Associates.

Sander, E.K. (1972) When are speech sounds learned? *Journal of Speech and Hearing Disorders, 37,* 55–63.

Shipley, K., & McAfee, J. G. (2008). *Assessment in speech-language pathology* (4th ed.). Clifton Park, NY: Delmar Cengage Learning.

Shriberg, L., & Kent, R. D. (2012). *Clinical phonetics* (4th ed.). Boston, MA: Pearson.

Singh, S., & Singh, K. (2006). *Phonetics: Principles and practices* (3rd ed.). San Diego, CA: Plural.

Smit, A. B., Hand, L., Freilinger, J. J. Bernthal, J. E., & Bird, A. (1990) The Iowa articulation norms project and its Nebraska replication. *Journal of Speech and Hearing Disorders, 55,* 779–798.

Templin, M.C. (1957). *Certain language skills in children. Institute of Child Welfare Monograph*

Series No. 26. Minneapolis, MN: University of Minnesota Press.

Wellman, B., Case, L., Mengert, I., & Bradbury, D. (1931) Speech sounds of young children. *State University of Iowa Studies in Child Welfare, 5*(2).

Online Resources

International Phonetic Association: https://www.internationalphoneticassociation.org/

International Phonetic Alphabet, promoting the study of phonetics: http://www.internationalphoneticalphabet.org/

Online Interactive Phonemic Learning: http://cambridgeenglishonline.com/Phonetics_Focus/

Using IPA symbols in documents with Unicode: http://www.phon.ucl.ac.uk/home/wells/ipa-unicode.htm

Audio files of IPA: http://web.uvic.ca/ling/resources/ipa/charts/IPAlab/IPAlab.htm

Sounds of Speech, module/app available: http://soundsofspeech.uiowa.edu/index.html#english

Douglass Phonetics Laboratory: http://dingo.sbs.arizona.edu/~dpl/

North American English Dialects, based on pronunciation patterns: http://aschmann.net/AmEng/

Index of American Dialects: http://www.evolpub.com/Americandialects

American Speech-Language and Hearing Association: https://www.asha.org/

American Cleft Palate Association: http://acpa-cpf.org/

Glossary

abduction: movement of vocal folds to open the space between the folds; folds do not vibrate

adduction: movement of vocal folds to close the space between the folds; folds vibrate

affricate: phonemes that begin with a stop consonant and end with production of a fricative, for example, /tʃ/ and /dʒ/

African American English: a dialect of English

alveolar ridge: structure located behind upper teeth; also known as the gum ridge

approximation: a position of closeness of the articulators that causes some constriction; associated with oral resonant consonants

articulation: modification of the breath stream by organs of the speech mechanism to produce speech

aspiration: release of impounded air for production of a stop-consonant

assimilation: a type of accommodation; produces major changes that occur when a phoneme is omitted, added, or changed to a different phoneme

bilabial: phonemes produced by contact of both lips, for example, /b/

bound morpheme: a morpheme that must be bound to another morpheme to convey meaning, for example, cats

broad transcription: transcription of sounds using IPA; no diacritics used

closed syllable: a syllable that contains a consonant in the final position

cluster: two or more adjacent consonants in the same syllable, for example, spring, blue, fast

coarticulation: a type of accommodation; produces minor changes in phonemes

coda: consonant(s) that appear after a vowel in a syllable; not all syllables contain a coda

cognate: phonemes made in the same place and manner of articulation; only voicing differs

consonant: sound produced with a complete or partially obstructed vocal tract

dentals: referring to the teeth

335

diacritic: symbol indicating a specific way a phoneme has been produced

diphthong: two vowels spoken in continuation; an onglide or off-glide

distinctive features: a system describing attributes of a phoneme that is required to differentiate one phoneme from another, for example, distinguishing feature of /k/ and /g/ is voicing

elision: omission of a phoneme in a word or phrase

epenthesis: addition of a phoneme

epiglottis: a structure that acts like a cover for the opening to the larynx to prevent food and drink from entering trachea

free morpheme: morpheme that can stand alone to convey meaning, for example, cat

fricative: consonants produced with partial blockage of the airstream, resulting in turbulence or friction

glide: a consonant produced with relatively unobstructed vocal tract, such as /w/j/r/

glottal: referring to the glottis

glottal stop: speech sound produced when vocal folds partially adduct to create buildup of air pressure; written as ʔ

glottis: space between the vocal folds

hard palate: anterior 2/3 of roof of the mouth, separates oral and nasal cavities

homorganic: sounds produced in the same place; /ŋ/ and /k/ and /g/ are homorganic

intervocalic: consonant located between two vowels, for example, cookie

IPA: International Phonetic Alphabet; specialized sound-symbol system that represents sounds of languages

labial: referring to the lips

labiodental: consonant produced with lower lip and upper central incisors, for example, /f/ and /v/

larynx: structure composed of cartilage and muscles; vocal folds are located in the larynx

lateral: sound produced with airstream directed around the sides of the tongue, for example, /l/

lax: vowel produced with reduced muscular effort

lingua: referring to the tongue; Latin for "tongue"

lingual frenum: small, white cord of tissue located on floor of oral cavity to midline of under surface of tongue blade

liquid: generic term for /r/ and /l/ consonants

lungs: respiratory organ that provides a breath stream for speech

mandible: lower jaw

maxilla: upper jaw

monophthong: single vowel sound

morpheme: minimal meaningful unit of language

narrow transcription: transcription of speech sounds that uses diacritics to indicate specific way a sound is produced

nucleus: part of the composition of a syllable, usually a vowel

obstruent: consonant produced with full or partial blockage of the vocal tract

off-glide: movement of tongue from lower to higher vowel (movement from vowel of longer duration to one of shorter duration) in diphthong production, for example, /au̯/

on-glide: diphthong movement from a preceding sound into a vowel of longer duration, for example, /ju̯/

onset: consonant that precedes a vowel in a syllable, for example, dog; not all syllables contain an onset

open syllable: syllable containing a vowel in final position, for example, go

palatal: consonants produced by body of tongue contacting or approximating the posterior portion of the hard palate, for example, /ʃ/ʒ/tʃ/dʒ/j/

PARR: reference to speech as an end product of four processes of *Phonation, Articulation, Respiration* and, *Resonation*

pharynx: tubular-shaped structure; serves as a resonating tract

phonation: adduction of vocal folds for voiced sounds

phoneme: speech sound that can be distinguished from other speech sounds

place of articulation: location of specific articulators used in production of a specific phoneme

postvocalic consonant: consonant that follows a vowel

prevocalic consonant: consonant that precedes a vowel

progressive assimilation: preceding phoneme influences a phoneme that follows; occurs left to right in an utterance

resonance: process of vibrating air in a resonating cavity, for example, oral or nasal cavity

respiration: flow of air from lungs; exhaled air is used for speech

rhyme: part of a syllable consisting of a nucleus and optional coda

SAE: (Standard American English) form of English that is "accent free"

sibilant: consonant produced with a "hissing" sound, such as /s/ or /ʃ/

sonorants: consonant produced by a relatively open vocal tract

stop consonant: consonant produced with complete obstruction of the airstream

syllabic consonant: consonant with a vowel-like quality

tap: also called "flap." Manner of production of consonant that is a rapid tongue movement against the alveolar ridge, that is, /ɾ/

tense: description of vowel produced by increased muscular effort

tongue advancement: used in the vowel quadrangle; refers to how far forward in the oral cavity the tongue is located; horizontal dimension of the VQ

tongue height: used in the vowel quadrangle; refers to tongue height in the vertical dimension of the VQ

trachea: cartilaginous tube composed of rings; connects larynx with lungs

transcription: using IPA symbols to represent speech sounds

velar: consonants produced when back portion of tongue contacts velum, for example, /k/g/ŋ/

velopharyngeal valve: composed of the velum and musculature of the posterior pharyngeal wall

velum: soft palate located posterior to the hard palate

vocal folds: folds of elastic tissue composed of muscles

voiced: phoneme produced with vocal fold vibration

voiceless: phoneme produced without vocal fold vibration

vowel: phoneme produced with relatively open vocal tract

vowel quadrangle (VQ): figure representing production of vowels with reference to tongue height and advancement in the oral cavity

Index